DATE DUE			JU 30
JUN			
APR 2 8 1992			

Rosa Bonheur

Rosa

A Life

A Studio Book

Bonheur
and a Legend

TEXT BY
Dore Ashton

ILLUSTRATIONS
AND CAPTIONS BY
Denise Browne Hare

The Viking Press   New York

First published in 1981 by The Viking Press
625 Madison Avenue, New York, N.Y. 10022

Published simultaneously in Canada by
Penguin Books Canada Limited

Library of Congress Cataloging in Publication Data
Ashton, Dore.
Rosa Bonheur: a life and a legend.
(A Studio book)
Bibliography: p. 197.
Includes index.
1. Bonheur, Rosa, 1822–1899.
2. Painters—France—Biography. I. Hare, Denise.
ND553.B6A9   759.4[B]   80-36749
ISBN 0-670-60813-0

Printed in the United States of America

Set in CRT Janson

Many of the works of art reproduced in this book are in the Musée de l'Atelier de Rosa Bonheur at the Château de By, France; their location is indicated in the captions as "Atelier, By." Since the museum was undergoing renovation during the time that this book was in preparation, the authors were unable in some cases to determine the exact dimensions of the works. For further information, the interested reader may write directly to the curator of the museum.

The present location of several other works is not known, as the captions indicate. The reproductions in these cases were obtained from Anna Klumpke, *Rosa Bonheur: Sa Vie, Son Oeuvre* (see Bibliography); this source is indicated in the captions as "Klumpke."

Modern photographs of the Rosa Bonheur Atelier were taken by Denise Browne Hare, who researched and selected the illustrations for this book.

PHOTOGRAPH ON THE FRONTISPIECE: Rue Rosa Bonheur in Paris was cut through in 1900 on the site of the old slaughterhouses of Grenelle along with a number of other streets named after artists: rue Vigée-Lebrun, rue de Staël, rue César Franck.

Acknowledgments

I am especially grateful to Professor Albert Boime for sharing his extensive research with me, for his invaluable publications, and for his generosity. I thank Professor Lorenz Eitner for his friendship and his excellent texts on Géricault. Professor Reinhold Heller first told me about Buffalo Bill's impact on artists in Paris, especially Munch and Gauguin, and Professor Robert Herbert helped me to wrestle with the question of Rosa Bonheur's background. Mme. C. Samoyault-Verlet graciously opened the Bonheur collection at the Musée National du Château de Fontainebleau to me.

—D.A.

To the Bernard Monnier family who first lured me to the Château de By—for their friendship, both past and present—I am forever grateful. Were it not for their instant enthusiasm, I doubt that this project would have been.

My thanks to Mr. Louis Sorrel-Dejèrine and family for their warm welcome to the Château de By and for giving me permission to photograph the Rosa Bonheur Atelier there.

To Catherine A. Mueller for her vivid recollections of her great-aunt, Anna Klumpke, and for giving me access to her Rosa Bonheur collection, I am most thankful.

At the Metropolitan Museum of Art, I am indebted to Margaretta Salinger for sharing her wide knowledge of the *Horse Fair* with me and to Doreen Burke for her study of Anna Klumpke.

To Dick Frost at the Buffalo Bill Museum in Cody, Wyoming; Joseph Rishel at the Philadelphia Museum of Art; Gilberte Martin-Mery at the Musée des Beaux-Arts in Bordeaux; J. Patrice Marandel at the Museum of Fine Arts in Houston; and Elizabeth E. Roth, Keeper of Prints, at the New York Public Library, who gave me their valued assistance, I am most grateful, as I am also to Madeleine Fidell-Beaufort, Beatrice Farwell, Monique Wust, and Jean Haritschelhar.

For their prompt responses to my queries, I thank the Wyoming State Historical Society and the Percheron Horse Society of America.

To Katharine Kuh for her encouragement and her talent to ferret out Bonheurs from the most unlikely of places, a very special thank you.

And to Rosalie Lanier—who gave me time for pause and thought.

—D.B.H.

We are especially grateful to our editor, Barbara Bullard Burn, whose affection for and knowledge of both art and animals made her collaboration particularly helpful and whose unflagging enthusiasm and encouragement urged us on.

—D.A. and D.B.H.

Foreword

DENISE BROWNE HARE

Rose Bonheur in Fontainebleau? I remember being bemused when I first heard her name reeled off with all those celebrated nineteenth-century artists who had been lured to this country-side by its infinite beauty. It was the springtime of 1977 and I had come to visit friends in the village of Villiers, nearby. That afternoon we were to go to her studio. Having until then given little thought to the habitat of this once-renowned painter of ani-mals, I suppose I would have placed her atelier close to a horse market, possibly near the Jardin des Plantes in Paris. But not here in Fontainebleau, a territory belonging to the partisans of the Barbizon School, who so ardently changed the silvery wild-woods and the misty fields into one of art's most familiar land-scapes. I was mistaken.

Not only had Rosa Bonheur lived and worked on the far side of the great Forest of Fontainebleau for some forty years, but, shortly after her death there in 1899, the town of Fontainebleau saw fit to erect, in a tranquil tree-lined square, a fitting monu-ment to its most illustrious citizen. The large-scale sculpture of a bull is gone today, melted down, along with many other notable bronze French figures, by the occupying German army during the 1940s. This public tribute to Bonheur and the tale of its de-mise had the clear ring of a metaphor to me. But back to the first heartbeat of this book.

Driving through the greening forest along the Route Ronde to the hamlet of By, I recall my companions telling me a bit about Rosa Bonheur—the usual blur of childhood memory and myth that has always encircled Rosa Bonheur's name. "She painted that extraordinary picture *The Horse Fair* with all those Percherons." "Yes, I remember an old litho of it hanging in my classroom when I was a child." "Didn't she go to America to paint Indians?" "She dressed like a man." "George Sand and Bonheur were friends." And so on. Was it because her paintings revealed so little of her personality, other than a lifelong love affair with the nature of animals, that she remained such an elusive figure? Or was forgetfulness just a built-in element of shifting fashions?

That afternoon, however, speculations such as these were sitting far back in my mind. My friends simply wanted to show me the curious old Bonheur place, overflowing with memorabilia mostly having to do with horses. Stuffed heads, plaster casts, paintings and sculptures, bridles, harnesses, even the artist's old riding saddle. They knew that I spent my summers in a mountain valley not far from Cody, Wyoming, and guessed that all this would connect with my own penchant for horses. Also, it seemed, on one of her studio walls hung an old Indian embroidered buckskin jacket similar to the one I was wearing that day. It was part of a small collection of Plains Indians artifacts given to her, according to legend, by none other than that flamboyant Indian scout and showman Buffalo Bill Cody. So this was where the "Colonel" had had his portrait painted by Rosa Bonheur? A romantic little painting I know well, it hangs among the Bierstadts, Catlins, Bodmers, Remingtons, and others in the Whitney Gallery of Western Art in Cody. "Buffalo Bill," drenched in bravado, riding his prancing white steed and sporting, naturally, a buckskin jacket just like mine.

Yet nothing could have quite prepared me for the scene that unfolded behind the high whitewashed walls of the estate. There stood an impressive manor house, the Château de By, with sprawling brick wings and turreted slate roofs. Beyond it, as far as one could see, appeared to be a large fragment of the Forest of Fontainebleau growing wild and dense within the walled boundaries. (There was little *déjà-vu* about this artist's country retreat. It did, though, conjure up for me a vision or two from Cocteau's film *Beauty and the Beast.* Lonely and mysterious.)

On climbing the small circular staircase leading to the wing in which the studio is located, I noted that the only light over the broken steps was filtered through a dusty round skylight overhead where the curling letters R.B. were entwined in deep blue glass, occupying its central pane. After scrambling over debris, piles of books, broken furniture, and old torn canvases, we went through a small side door to the inner sanctuary: the Rosa Bonheur Atelier. It was a sight, a total wreck of a place, astonishing and awful all at once.*

Sometimes a thing seems too big to be grasped in its entirety, and, in an effort to make some sense out of it, one searches for pieces so that the whole may come into focus. So, with the permission of our host, I started to record with my camera—crowded tabletops, unfinished paintings, her old black velvet jacket with the faded Légion d'Honneur rosette still in its buttonhole, the carved stone hunting dogs supporting the huge mantelpiece, cluttered étagères, walls heavy with animal trophies, the marvelous mess of it all—in the hope that the photographs would, later on, put some order into my understanding of this strange place.

A few weeks later, back at home, conjuring with the thoughts and fancies this visit had sprung on me, I went to see my close friend Dore Ashton. I had the photographs in hand, and Dore was intrigued. Yes, this was a matter to pursue. The Rosa Bonheur story had most of the elements necessary to shape an interesting book: myth, contradiction, timeliness, ambiguity, changing values, and even humor. We set about sketching an approach to our collaboration. It would be a two-part work, presented in different voices, one written and one illustrated. The structure would be set around themes rather than chronology because it was evident that Bonheur's rise to fame was made possible not by talent alone but rather by a changing society. She was born under lucky stars.

History, the arts, sociology, philosophy, the natural sciences, economics—all have a place in understanding why it was possi-

* Since my first visit to the Château de By, the Atelier has been completely restored and is now open to the public.

ble for Rosa Bonheur to become the international celebrity that she was. We would investigate how these areas of inquiry affected her development as an artist and most especially how she took advantage of the new options open to her. To be an eccentric and a maverick; to be single-minded and ambitious; to produce a large body of work—these were some of the possibilities no longer limited to the male sex.

After her death there surfaced more than the usual number of reminiscences that echo the obituaries of the famed, more than could be attributed to her talent as a painter or to her feminist position. Some memoirs, no doubt, were imaginary. The following homage, supposedly written by Victor Hugo about Rosa Bonheur, is one of these. It appeared as the introduction to a quaint recollection by one Elbert Hubbard in his book *Little Journeys to the Homes of Famous Women:*

> The boldness of her conception is sublime. As a Creative Artist I place her first among women, living or dead. And if you ask me why she thus towers above her fellows, by the majesty of her work silencing every detractor, I will say it is because she listens to God and not to man. She is the true self.

What was it about Rosa Bonheur that brought out the extravagant adulation and public interest? What was it that attracted such fascination seemingly out of proportion to her personality and her talent?

In an attempt to illuminate this paradox, Dore and I set up two mirrors, one marked "history," the other "personality." They were set facing each other, reflecting back and forth. Our hope was that Rosa Bonheur would take shape in the space between. What did take shape was an individual, an original whose life and work seemed to coincide with a need in others, both in her time and in ours, a nineteenth-century woman so strong-willed and directed that nearing her death she was able to reflect on her long life as an artist with this statement:

> Art is a tyrant. It demands heart, brain, soul, body. The entireness of the votary. Nothing less will win its highest favor. I wed art. It is my husband, my world, my life dream, the air I breathe. I know nothing else, feel nothing else, think nothing else.

Contents

Rosa Bonheur

1.
Bonheur *Père*

Throughout her life, Rosa Bonheur ceaselessly reviewed her childhood, attempting to compose a satisfactory image from its hectic, often disrupted sequence. Her father, Raimond Oscar-Marie Bonheur, a modestly successful artist, exercised enough authority to make all four of his children artists, and he took his place in her memory as the strongest formative influence in her life. Her artistic success, she always told interviewers, was entirely due to his tenacity and faith. You will surpass Mme. Vigée-Lebrun, he used to tell her. (In her late memoirs, RB added to his prophecy: "You will surpass Mme. Vigée-Lebrun of the Royal Academy, the Rome Academy, the St. Petersburg Academy, and the Berlin Academy.") Although in many ways a quixotic and inconsistent person, Raimond Bonheur was a firm mentor whose ambitions were projected through his children. Despite her ambivalence about his character, RB remained in her own mind a product of her father's intense ambition.

In allusions to Raimond Bonheur in various memoirs, writers have spoken in a tone of indulgent admiration for his innate charm. RB herself could never resist telling friends with pride that her father, with his golden ringlets and ingratiating manner, was known in his native city of Bordeaux as "The Angel Gabriel." In her accounts, he emerged as an irresistible if somewhat impressionable *charmeur* in his relations with others. She usually began her description of her father by telling of his youthful success as a drawing master in Bordeaux and then she

Raimond Oscar-Marie Bonheur: *Self-portrait.* Oil, ca. 1823. Klumpke. ❧ "The only thing noble about my parents was their character," Rosa would say proudly about their simple origins, "which is more than many so-called aristocrats can boast."

would quickly bring him to Paris, avoiding as much as possible the facts of his humble origin.

According to his marriage certificate, Raimond was born in 1796 the son of François Bonheur, who was recorded as being "without profession," and Marie Pérar, but in later years RB and her family sought to provide a respectable family history and established Raimond as the son of the last of a long line of pastry chefs. According to his grandnephew who had done the research, Raimond's father had been employed as head chef of an important Toulouse family, the Cambacères, in whose kitchen the gifted child Raimond was said to have done his first drawings "by imitating the ornaments in butter and sugar his father executed." There is no evidence for this other than the nephew's claim, and for purely geographical reasons it seems, in any case, an unlikely story, since Raimond was sent by his family to study at a drawing school in the province of Bordeaux.

The school Raimond attended was headed by an eccentric minor artist, Pierre Lacour (1778–1859), who had been a pupil of David. He dabbled in archaeology and philology, and his reactionary aesthetic views strongly influenced the young Raimond. A hint of Lacour's provincial resistance to the upheavals in the Parisian art world is found in Raimond Bonheur's letter to his old master written years later: "It was due to you that I turned my back on the dangerous doctrines of Boulanger and company."

The doctrines expounded by the painter Louis Boulanger that were regarded so mistrustfully by Lacour and his pupil were mostly those of Boulanger's close friend Victor Hugo. Boulanger had been one of a band of young painters, among them Delacroix, who had looked to Hugo for leadership and inspiration. Hugo's forceful temperament abetted them in their struggle to find a way out of the dilemma experienced so keenly by the artists of the post-Napoleonic generation. The studios were filled with rebellious youths who felt themselves embattled. They could no longer accept the neoclassic tradition in painting in spite of the appealing radical political intonation supplied by Jacques-Louis David. They had been smitten by Géricault's audacity when he exhibited *The Raft of Medusa* in 1819 and sensed that he had laid the groundwork for a new style—a style still politically progressive but not bound by the formal austerities of the neoclassic heritage. Many of these young art students were deeply disappointed with the return of monarchy after the excitement of the Napoleonic era and were seeking not only a new expression in their painting, but also a framework for their point of view. Hugo, with his immense capacity for persuasion, became the agent of their definitive break with received ideas in painting. He gathered around him dozens of young poets and painters who were only too eager to embrace his newly formulated theory of romanticism. It was Boulanger, rather than the more prominent Delacroix, who drew the wrath of Raimond's teacher Lacour, probably because he was more voluble and because his literary friends (including Hugo, Sainte-Beuve, Gérard de Nerval, Gautier, and Balzac) admired him so often in the journals and newspapers that reached the provinces. When the news traveled outside Paris in the early years of the romantic movement, Boulanger may well have seemed the sinister initiator merely because he was so closely allied with Hugo.

Raimond, then, was saved from the iniquities of the Parisian art world long before he went to Paris in 1828. He described himself in his marriage certificate as a classical "history painter" at a time when history painting was associated with the bypassed neoclassic canon. His artistic conservatism, instilled by Lacour, was still apparent years later when he wrote proudly of his daughter's accomplishment in taking first prize in the Salon of 1848. "Rejoice," he told Lacour, "because she is, in a way, your student. Didn't I transmit to her the ideal of the beautiful that you taught, and the methods of serious study that have preserved her from the capricious tastes of those who pass quickly out of sight with their extreme ways of trying to be original?"

Despite Lacour's conservatism in art, he may well have been the one who started Raimond in his quest for a Utopian socialist vision of universal harmony. Lacour in his later years wrote tracts promoting ancient religions and seems to have taken some extreme positions. His pamphlet "God or the Gods of Moses" earned him the implacable hatred of the Catholic Church, and he was placed on the Index. Raimond in his letters consoled his old teacher and promised him that his ideals would one day be realized through art and that he would see his grateful students "project a line of conscientious artists who would not seek by petty means the ovation of the world."

At the same time that Raimond was assimilating Lacour's views, he was exposed to a unique situation in Bordeaux that had little to do with the traditionalism of the Academy. During the years of his artistic formation, Bordeaux was host to a large colony of artists and intellectuals from Spain, most of whom had fled after Napoleon had failed to impose his liberalization there. These refugees preserved a vivid cultural life that did not fail to impress the local students. Some of RB's strongest memories of her early childhood were connected with one of the most prominent of the Spanish émigrés, the playwright Leandro Fernandez de Moratín (1760–1828). This author of numerous plays as well as an important history of the origins of Spanish theater had accepted the post of Royal Librarian under Joseph Bonaparte and had been forced to flee in 1814. He was a frequent guest in the home of RB's grandfather, where he used to play hide-and-seek with RB, admire her early drawings, and call her his "little ball."

It is possible that the Bonheurs may have encountered Goya at this time. Goya had first painted his friend Moratín's portrait in 1799 and again in 1824 in Bordeaux. Goya visited Moratín immediately after he arrived in France and, as Moratín wrote, "dined with us as if he were a young student." Moratín reported in 1825 that Goya was "pleased with the city, the countryside, the climate, and the food." It seems likely that the Bonheur family met Goya at one of Moratín's dinners, judging from one of

Francisco de Goya: *Leandro Fernandez de Moratín.* Oil, 1824. Museum of Fine Arts, Bilbao. ❧ Goya painted this portrait of his friend, the distinguished Spanish poet and playwright, while they were both living in exile in Bordeaux. In 1827 Moratín went to Paris to join the Manuel Silvela family, who were friends and benefactors of Raimond Bonheur, and he died there the following year. He was buried in the Père Lachaise cemetery, next to Molière and La Fontaine. In due time his remains were returned to Spain, there to be buried in the same crypt with Goya's.

Raimond's wife's letters dated August 20, 1828, shortly after Raimond had left for Paris:

> You must know that poor Goya went and died a few days ago, and what surprised me was that the man they had for a long time left in the most profound poverty had a funeral of a prince.

While there is little in Raimond's history that reflects any direct influence of the artistic Spanish colony in Bordeaux, the social connections with such prominent Spaniards were eventually to stand the whole family in good stead. More than fifty years later, RB attributed her official honors from Queen Isabella to her father's early associations with the Spanish intellectual aristocracy.

2.
Bonheur *Mère*

One of Raimond's pupils in Bordeaux after he became a successful young drawing master was a girl named Sophie Marquis. Sophie had been brought up in the home of Jean Baptiste Dublan de Lahet, a merchant in Bordeaux who had known better times. According to RB's last reminiscences, he was the son of a financier who had been Treasurer during the reign of Louis XV, and had been a page of Marie Antoinette, but little else is known about him. For some reason he had fetched Sophie from Altona, Germany, where she had been born in 1797 and registered as the legitimate child of Laurent-Modeste-Antoine Marchisio, called Marquis, and Marie-Anne Triling. She was two years old when she entered M. Dublan's household, where she was called his "niece" and "pupil." M. Dublan raised her with his own children and supervised her studies of French literature, composition, piano, dance, and drawing.

RB later recalled witnessing many domestic scenes of exceptional harmony in the Dublan household, among them the image of her mother at the harpsichord accompanying M. Dublan on the flute. Sophie's "uncle" took a dim view of her infatuation with the drawing master Bonheur and resisted her desire to marry him. But, since it was a love match, he eventually assented, and on May 21, 1821, they were married with his blessings. The following year, on March 16, Sophie gave birth to a daughter, whom they christened Rosalie.

In M. Dublan's comfortable bourgeois home, Sophie had had an education that suited her for a life sharply differing from any-

(LEFT) Raimond Bonheur: *Sophie Bonheur with her children Auguste and Rosa*. Drawing, 1827. Klumpke. ❀ "A veil hangs over her birth," Rosa said in an interview, describing her mother's origins.

(BELOW) Jean Baptiste Dublan de Lahet and a copy of his death certificate, 1830. ❀ It is said that M. Dublan, Sophie Bonheur's guardian, confessed to Rosa's mother on his deathbed that he was her true father.

thing young Raimond could offer her. His own bitter references in later years to his exceedingly humble origins indicate that he always felt at a disadvantage. While he was proud to be a "son of the people," he evidently regarded his status as a hindrance to the fulfillment of his artistic ideals. Sophie, emerging from a cultured milieu, endeavored to amplify his knowledge of the world. She had access to the cultured classes in Bordeaux and, in her girlhood, had frequented the homes of both the local French gentry and the Spanish. She exposed Raimond to the wider world of arts and letters and introduced him to people who would eventually help him. When he later went to Paris he was received by the Spanish family Silvela, who, along with the Figueras and Moratín, had been close friends of Sophie. (Manuel Silvela, who had lived in Bordeaux in Sophie's youth, had been with the Court of Joseph Bonaparte and was painted by Goya in Paris.)

It is obvious in RB's tremulous accounts that she saw her mother as a fine-grained aristocrat unjustly condemned to a life

(RIGHT) Raimond Bonheur: *The Infant Rosa Bonheur*. Oil, 1823. Klumpke. ❧ Other than a few drawings and paintings of his wife and children, little remains of Raimond Bonheur's oeuvre.

(BELOW) Rosa Bonheur's birth certificate. ❧ She was born in Bordeaux on March 16, 1822. Her given name was inscribed as Rosalie although she was always to be known as Rosa. Her paternal grandfather, François Bonheur, a cook, was witness, but being illiterate he was unable to sign the document.

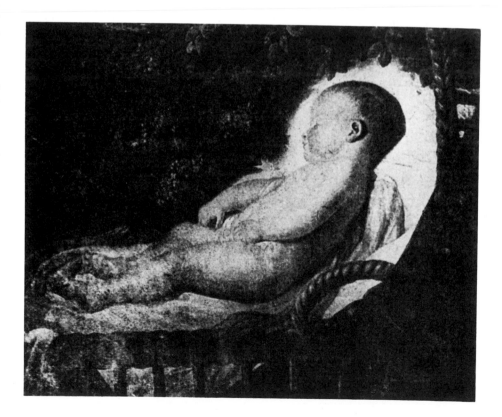

of material deprivation and unfulfilled aspirations. Although Sophie was listed on her marriage certificate as "daughter of an unknown father and mother," Rosa clung to the hope that one day she could prove her mother's noble birth. At the end of her life, dictating her autobiography to her companion, Anna Klumpke, she related that on his deathbed in 1830 M. Dublan had summoned Sophie and announced that she was his daughter. When she asked him about her mother, he replied, "I promised never to reveal it, but you will find in my writing desk papers which will tell you." Alas, the writing desk had been rifled, leaving Sophie disinherited and ignorant of her mother's origins. As RB grew older, she persisted in believing that somewhere she would find proof of her mother's high birth; she even believed that certain aristocrats who had become her patrons might have known the secret.

There is not much documentation to support RB's final version of Sophie's origins, but there is considerable evidence in RB's comments and autobiographical sketches that she had formed an especially strong attachment to her mother, who died when she was only eleven years old. This goaded RB to explore every avenue in the search for more information concerning Sophie's background. After her great success and her concourse with royalty, RB even hypothesized that an elevated position on the social scale had been the cause of her rise to fame. "The marks of esteem which I have received at different epochs from several crowned heads are such that I cannot, in conscience, attribute them uniquely to my talent," she told Klumpke.

In her earlier recollections, RB remembered her mother proudly as the protégée of a rich family who had willingly, through love, undertaken the arduous lot of a poor artist's wife. But at times her mother's despair seemed to RB the result of her submission to an impoverished life. At other times RB draws the portrait of a beautiful, idealistic woman who cheerfully undertook her responsibilities and shared her husband's rather extravagant social ideals. She relates how, in the early years of their marriage, Sophie had been obliged to live with Raimond's parents, *Pépé* and *Mémé* as they were called in Bordelaise, and how she had adapted valiantly to these very simple people. Because Sophie had had a child only a year after her wedding and another, Auguste, in the following year, Raimond found it increasingly difficult to support his family, and Sophie was obliged to help out by giving music lessons to local children. All the same, she was an attentive and tender mother, and RB speaks repeatedly of her contentment in her mother's company.

Sophie had early encouraged Rosa to draw, and when the child had difficulty learning to read she devised an ingenious scheme for teaching her. "One day she had a bright idea," RB relates. "She told me to draw an ass opposite the A and a cow opposite the C and so on." In this way RB learned the alphabet and at the same time learned to interpret the world through animal images. Sophie kept all of Rosa's childish drawings and offered them at times to friends, among them Moratín, who is said to have cherished the pictures.

RB's memory of her childhood in Bordeaux is centered on her mother. Her descriptions of their ramblings in the cultivated gardens of friends' country estates suggest a lost paradise perpetually regretted. Despite their poverty, Sophie clearly attempted to raise her first child as she herself had been raised. She would sit with RB in the evenings, often singing to her at the piano. She kept afternoons for their work with the alphabet and constantly sought to stimulate the child's artistic faculties. "I was allowed to run about everywhere," RB wrote in one of her late autobiographical sketches, "and I have kept the sweetest recollection of that happy time of freedom."

> I covered the white walls with my shapeless sketches as high as I could reach, and also enjoyed myself very much in cutting out paper models. They were invariably the same; first I made long strips of paper, then with my scissors I cut out the shepherd, then the dog, then the cow, the sheep, and finally the tree, always in the same order.

RB's very early interest in animals was evident to her mother, who proudly spoke of the child's animal drawings and permitted her to spend happy hours in M. Dublan's country estate, where, as RB remembered with amusement, she frequented the stables. "I had for the stables a more irresistible taste than ever a courtesan for the royal or imperial antechambers."

Raimond Bonheur: *Rosa at Four*. Oil, 1826. Atelier, By. ✿ Hugging her *polichinelle* marionette, Rosa is dressed in a costume similar to the one she was to favor during most of her life.

Jean Baptiste Corot: *Portrait of Rosa Bonheur as a Child.* Oil on wood,
ca. 1835. Metropolitan Museum of Art, New York. ❧ Although "little Father Corot," as Rosa called him, was a much admired friend of the Bonheur
family, the circumstances under which this portrait was painted are
not known.

But Rosa also retained memories of her mother's exhaustion as she struggled to feed a growing brood of children (Isidore was born in 1827 and Juliette in 1830), and she composed an angelic image of Sophie as physically beautiful, patient, filled with love and good will for her volatile and restless husband. Rosa often told close friends how her mother appeared to her in dreams, sweetly encouraging her bereft daughter and promising to be a guardian angel. This dream recurred even in RB's last years, for the grief she had experienced when her mother had died in 1833 was permanent. RB identified her own emotional difficulties with the early loss of her mother and seemed to recognize that her attachments to women rather than men had in some way been affected by her perception of her parents' troubled life.

3.
Raimond Bonheur, Apostle

Raimond Bonheur, his daughter once said with a hint of bitterness, "had the temperament of an apostle." He conceived fervent enthusiasms that he found hard to forsake even when they imposed hardships on his family. In Bordeaux he had been turned away from the "dangerous doctrines" of Louis Boulanger and Victor Hugo only to find the more dangerous doctrines of the burgeoning socialist utopian movements. When RB was barely six years old, Raimond decided to follow his sister Elizabeth and the Silvela family to Paris probably as much to find new socialist milieus as to further his artistic ambitions. He left his wife behind with the three children and promised to send for them as soon as he had a job. Although accounts are somewhat confused as to his first steps toward becoming a true "disciple," it seems that he quickly encountered other young men questing for a cause to fill the spiritual vacuum left by Napoleon.

During his first lonely year in Paris from March 1828 to April 1829, Raimond cast about for companionship and for an outlet for his innate idealism. He found both in the company of young political dissidents rather than in the art world. Before his commitment to the Saint-Simonians, he frequented the group around Pierre-Jean Béranger, an ardent Bonapartist whose popular songs, "Chansons Morales et Autres," had landed him in prison in 1821 and again in 1828. Béranger's followers included young workers who met regularly to discuss their publication, the *Ruche Populaire*, and whose general attitude of disaffection suited Raimond's mood.

Raimond Bonheur: *Rosa and Her Brother Auguste.* Oil, 1827. Musée des Beaux-Arts, Bordeaux. ✤ The little portrait of Raimond's growing family reflects a strict fidelity to his neoclassical training.

Leclerc: *Barthélemy-Prosper Enfantin*. Lithograph, 1832. ❧ "*Le Père Enfantin*" took leadership of the Saint-Simonians in 1825 upon the death of the founder, le Comte de Saint-Simon. Rosa Bonheur's father, restless, impulsive, and a dreamer by nature, was an ideal candidate for this religious socialist utopian sect, which he joined in 1828.

From a letter to a school friend in Bordeaux written March 1, 1831, we get a glimpse of Raimond's confusion in his early Paris days:

Like you, my dear Durand, and with the greatest energy, I have cried in the desert—cries of imprecations and sorrow against a blind power which seems to conduct everything cruelly into the yawning mouth of fatality, the fiend of ruin and destruction which tears us all apart all the more unmercifully because we are generous and tender! I revolted and strongly protested against every belief except that of my own individual conscience.... I was in a state of despairing skepticism when a friendly voice directed me to the doctrines of Saint-Simon.... I read much, I meditated long on the works explaining the doctrine and I attended lectures. One evening I argued with all my forces against everything that appeared to me Utopian, dreamy, anarchical, and Jesuitical. It seemed to me that I saw contradictory tendencies on all sides. But I finally came to recognize that the apparent confusion emanated from myself....

In the 1820s when he began to gather disciples Saint-Simon had proposed that the new society would be based on the tenets that man first feels, then thinks, then acts. The richest source of feeling, he concluded, was still religion. Louis Blanc, in his alert eyewitness account *The History of Ten Years, 1830–1840*, sums up Saint-Simon's position shortly before his death:

Thus in the opinion of Saint-Simon, the *religious* power would have been that which embracing humanity in all that which constitutes its essence should have guided it towards that which forms the true aim and scope of Christianity, the amelioration of the lot of the most numerous, and by these three means: by feeling, employing therein the artist; by reason, employing therein the savants; by acts, employing therein men of labor.

Saint-Simon had high hopes in 1825, the last year of his life. He told his disciples, "The pear is ripe; pluck it." Immediately after his death his most faithful adherents set about promulgating his doctrine by founding a journal, *Le Producteur*, in which Olinde Rodrigues and Saint-Amand Bazard forged the Saint-

Simonian doctrine to which Raimond was susceptible. It could be summed up, as Louis Blanc noted, in three formulas:

—Universal association based on love. As a corollary, no more hostile competition.

—To each according to his capacity, to each capacity according to its work. The corollary: inherited property would be abolished.

—Organization of industry. The corollary: No more wars.

(Rodrigues added that there would be a central bank controlled by the industrials which would initiate great public works such as networks of railways to unite humanity and canals at Suez and Panama.)

These themes, published daily in several small journals, were also developed in an extended series of lectures by Bazard from 1828 through 1829—the period when Raimond probably attended. Louis Blanc found Bazard's logic wanting. He tartly pointed out that the Saint-Simonians tried to offer something to everybody. To orators they promised "a noble arena." Poets and artists were tempted with the bait of easily acquired reputations. Savants were taught the false and hollow nature of the existing science of liberalism, and women were courted with talk about the fine arts, love, and civil liberty.

While Blanc described Bazard's lectures as quiet and modest, attended by some thirty serious young people, the activities of the adepts after the July revolution became far more hectic. Spurred by their successes in 1829 and fired by their future leader, Barthélemy-Prosper Enfantin, the group issued a proclamation demanding the common ownership of goods, abolition of inheritance, and the enfranchisement of women. They strongly emphasized the role of feeling, and indeed, feelings seemed to have been deliberately inflamed by the leaders. A spiritually hungry youth such as Raimond Bonheur thrilled to what Blanc called the "mighty harangues" offered in 1830 at the rue Taitbout:

Nothing could be more curious than the spectacle presented by these assemblies. Around a vast hall, beneath a roof of glass, there

LA TENTATION DE SAINT-SIMON.

The Temptation of Saint-Simon. Cartoon, 1832. ❧ "Trouble your heads not with the affairs of this wretched world of ours" is the advice given to the Saint-Simonians by a contemporary wag ridiculing their lofty, visionary, and unrealistic beliefs.

arose three tiers of boxes. On the stage in front of these and an ample pit, the benches of which, as the clock struck twelve, were crowded with an eager audience, there arranged themselves every Sunday, seated in three rows, a number of young and serious-looking men habited in blue, among whom might be seen also a few ladies dressed in white, with violet-colored scarves. By and by there appeared, leading forward the preacher of the day, the two supreme fathers of the society, Messieurs Bazard and Enfantin. As they advanced to the front, the disciples rose with looks of tender veneration; while among the spectators there immediately prevailed an intense silence, contemplative or ironical. . . .

These sober meetings soon gave way to interior squabbles in which Bazard and Enfantin became increasingly estranged. The young Polytechnicians and a few of the more distinguished literary men who had listened for months to their diatribes, and who had even consented to become a "family" under the tutelage of the two fathers, began to worry about Enfantin's somewhat mystical tendencies. His radical proposals concerning equality of men and women seemed to some as "legalized adultery." Finally there was a painful schism leaving Enfantin the leader of the remaining disciples.

Among some seventy-nine of the faithful was the impressionable Raimond, who by this time was reunited with his wife and three children and struggling to keep bread on the table. RB recalled with suppressed anger her father's exclusive passion for the Saint-Simonian "family" while he neglected the needs of his own. Those were the days when Sophie Bonheur was strained to the breaking point. Every day, for instance, she had to travel great distances to Les Halles to find cheaper vegetables. She sought to sustain the family as much as possible by giving music lessons, but these proved inadequate and she was forced to work late at night doing piecework, mostly sewing ladies' fancy garters.

Meanwhile, Enfantin, who was now called "Père," gathered the faithful in a monkish retreat in Ménilmontant, to which Raimond attached himself along with some seventy others in 1831. As yet the disciples were still "in the world," and both Sophie and Raimond were enlisted as missionaries in one of the four

LES MOINES DE MÉNILMONTANT
ou
LES CAPACITÉS SAINT-SIMONIENNES.

sections of Paris designated by Père Enfantin. As Enfantin's ambitions grew, so did Raimond's fervor. In 1832 Enfantin was proclaiming the social equality of men and women and speaking of "the rehabilitation of the needs and pleasures of the flesh" while planning to enforce monastic rules on his dwindling band of followers. By this time the Saint-Simonians styled themselves members of a Church with Fathers and Apostles and a willing band of monks to do the work, among them Raimond.

Fortunately for the Bonheur family, the monastery as a closed society had a very short existence. It commenced in April 1832, when Enfantin sequestered some forty of his disciples. They had accepted his latest notion that in accordance with the proclaimed principle of sexual equality, the new Church would

Image d'Epinal: *The Monks of Ménilmontant.* Lithograph, 1832. Klumpke. ⚜ This scene shows the "apostles" of Saint-Simon working at various tasks in their Paris retreat. Each member's former profession is listed after his present occupation: cook, vegetable parer, dishwasher, bootblack, laundryman, garbageman. Rosa Bonheur's father is registered as Gardener, formerly Professor of Drawing and Painting. He is shown in the foreground with a shovel.

19

have to await the arrival of a "Mother" to wed the "Father," symbolizing the marriage of feeling and intellect. At first Enfantin tried to entice George Sand to play "Mother," but she firmly rebuffed him, commenting to a friend that it would really be interpreting her works badly to find in them the profession of any sort of doctrine. When Sand failed him, Enfantin began to dream about a "Mother" who would be a Jewish woman coming from Turkey. Meanwhile, until "the Mother revealed herself," his followers were to remain celibate. Life in the monastery was described by one historian as follows:

> The brothers arose at five, breakfasted at seven, dined at one, supped at seven, and were in bed by ten. There were no domestics and each apostle had certain menial duties to perform. Thus the cultivated Gustave d'Eichthal cleaned plates, while the Father Superior presided over the garden, and among the brothers who aided him in the horticultural tasks was Raimond Bonheur....

On Wednesdays families and special guests were permitted to visit, and on Sundays there was open house.

During the summer of 1832 the monastery, with its inhabitants wearing their newly designed habits (probably designed by Raimond), became notorious. Both the curious and the hostile flocked to observe it. As many as ten thousand came to get a glimpse of the sect, and on occasion the government was forced to call out the army to avoid disorders. Louis-Philippe's ministers quickly grew wary as Enfantin drew increasing attention to his radical doctrines. Finally, late in August, the government invoked article 291, a repressive law that contributed to the Bourgeois King's fall nineteen years later:

> No association numbering more than 20 persons, which meets daily or on certain fixed dates, and whose aim is of a religious, literary, political, or other nature, can be formed without the consent of the government or under conditions other than those which it pleases the public authorities to impose on it.

On August 27 and 28, with the entire brotherhood present in their full regalia, the brothers were tried and the leaders duly condemned to fines and imprisonment. The following October they were again tried, this time for fiscal improprieties. Although they were later acquitted, their affairs were in serious disarray, and by late fall, when Enfantin and his chief lieutenants went to prison, the monastery had to be disbanded and Raimond returned home, still sworn, however, to further proselytizing activities. But, as RB recounted, the extreme poverty of the household made it almost impossible for him to give much time to the cause. "He resented it greatly, and several times in his moments of exaltation, I heard him say that only the Catholic Church could understand men and women who want to consecrate themselves to a great cause and must remain celibate."

Whenever Raimond railed thus against his fate his wife wept and clutched her older daughter to herself convulsively. This painful experience left RB with a lifelong ambivalence toward the man who could so unfeelingly consecrate himself to large abstractions while his own family bore the weight. Her reactions to Raimond's extravagantly sentimental commitments appear frequently in her memoirs, and sometimes she spoke proudly of his idealistic nature and the extremes to which it brought him. She described the Sunday visits to the monastery during the spring and summer with evident pride:

> Every Sunday we all went to pay him a visit at the "convent." The street boys would sometimes mock my Saint-Simonian cap with its big tassel. Some of them even threw stones at us. This touch of persecution made us all the more ardent supporters of the sect where my father made the acquaintance of such men as the Pereires, Arles-Dufour, Carnot, father of the future President, Le Verrier, Talabot, d'Eichthal, Enfantin, Michel Chevalier, Stephane Flachat, Olinde Rodrigues, Bazard, Auguste, Comte, and Félicien David, the composer, all superior minds in different fields. . . . This Saint-Simonian episode in our life had influences that I now perceive were much more far-reaching than any of us imagined at the time. . . .

Of her more positive feelings about Raimond's discipleship RB spoke freely in her late memoirs. She admired him for having designed the Saint-Simonian habit: a short violet-blue frock coat without a collar, a red vest fastened in back in order that no

(LEFT) Image d'Epinal: *Daily Occupations of Saint-Simonians.* Lithograph, 1832. ✤ Saint-Simonian cooking. Saint-Simonian mending.

(RIGHT) Image d'Epinal: *The Saint-Simonian Costume.* Lithograph, 1832. ✤ "White—the trousers—is to signify love; red—the vest—work; blue-violet—the frock-coat—faith," wrote Raimond Bonheur to his old teacher, Lacour, about the costume he had designed for the Saint-Simonians. "The whole costume symbolizes therefore that Saint-Simonianism is based on love, is fortified by labor, and is enveloped in faith."

The vest represented fraternity since it laced up the back, making the assistance of one of the "brothers" a must.

brother could dress himself without the aid of another, white trousers with a black leather belt and a brass buckle. RB also respected her father's views on the "regeneration of humanity" and sometimes spoke with warmth of his "universal benevolence." On one occasion she told Anna Klumpke, "Although he loved us with all the impetuosity of his character, what he sought above all was the amelioration of society." But on another occasion her resentment revealed itself clearly: "Oh! those beautiful words! They were never absent. In difficult moments, my father had a veritable eloquence. . . ." Still, she directed Klumpke to a pamphlet titled "The Notebook of the Theo-gyn-odemophile" which Raimond had published in 1833 and which, she explained, meant "the friend of God, woman, and of the people." In it Raimond spoke of religion, politics, and morality as representing the natural will toward the well-being and health of all. He lamented party dissensions and, in the last paragraph, earnestly preached in inflated and confused diction that the real evil in the world was that not enough people recognized the power of good will.

The pamphlet was published at a time when Raimond may already have been listening to the lucubrations of a rather different sect. Since half of the brothers had taken themselves off to Egypt or Greece or Turkey to lay the foundations for Père Enfantin's great engineering schemes, Raimond was relatively isolated. With his disciple's nature, he was sorely in need of consolation after the failure of the Ménilmontant experiment and the death of his wife, and he soon found a new doctrine in the Templiers. Unlike his fellow Saint-Simonians such as Hippolyte Carnot who had tried the Templiers *before* attaching to Saint-Simon and had found that "they were no more accessible to progress than Roman cardinals," Raimond found his way to the Templiers afterward. In one of his many changes of domicile, he moved into the quarter where the famous Café Parnassus sheltered a number of bohemian and radical regulars under the benevolent eye of an old carpenter whose claim to fame was that his daughter had married the famous Danton. There Raimond encountered Fabre-Palaprat, a physicist who had dabbled in experiments with electricity and who called himself the Grand

Master of the Templiers. Apparently Raimond was easily swayed by his rhetoric and was soon initiated into the secrets of the old sect. RB in her autobiographical memoir tells of this period in her father's life:

> This Palaprat had in his house the helmet and breast-plate of Jacques de Molay, the famous grand master of the order who was burnt by Philippe le Bel on the Pont Neuf in 1314. I need hardly say that my father took up the order formerly so severely persecuted by the cruel king of France. It was always his nature to be with the underdog. He carried his enthusiasm so far that I was baptised by the Knights of the Temple. . . . Among the souvenirs of their ancient glory, they had preserved their altar, their pulpit, and their baptismal fount. The ceremony was performed in their sort of chapel, under a canopy of steel formed by the drawn swords of the knights in costume, and, full of solemnity, it appealed eloquently to my imagination, so that for a time I believed myself a knight in reality.

The officers wore white robes and carried scarlet crosses, and at the end of the ceremony they gave her a wooden sword that would later bring her to grief in one of the pensions where her father subsequently tried to educate her.

It is clear that the experience with the Saint-Simonians and later with the Templiers made RB wary of all collective institutions. She had suffered ostracism, persecution, and poverty as a result of her father's discipleship, and she had seen her parents' marriage founder. The feelings she formed during this crucial period were divided, and all through her life the clash of values occurring in her own household would make her vacillate from one extreme to another.

Rosa Bonheur dressed as a Templier. Ca. 1837. Klumpke. ❧ "One day my father came to fetch me at boarding-school and took me that evening to the '*Chapelle des Cavaliers*' in the Court of Miracles to have me re-baptized as a little '*Templière*' as it was called in the language of that mystical order," Rosa recalled in her memoirs. "Naturally, I understood absolutely nothing . . . but I imagined I had been transfigured." Now and again she would dress up in the costume of the Templiers for fun.

4.
Early Years in Paris

In 1829 Sophie took her three children, Rosalie (age seven), Auguste (not quite five), and Isidore (almost two), in the coach to Paris—a journey of two days and three nights. She faced a precarious existence there. Although Raimond had found work at a boys' boarding school and gave a few private drawing lessons, his earnings were meager and intermittent. RB's salient memories of her first years in Paris were of frequent moves from one mean apartment to the next, and of pervasive economic anxiety. She keenly felt the loss of the idyllic life her family had known in Bordeaux. In her late years RB mentioned to nearly everyone who interviewed her the difficulty she had had adjusting to life in Paris: "I didn't like the great capital. Even the bread seemed insipid when compared to our southern loaves, which were salty and so to my taste." But she also emphasized the powerful effect that those first years in Paris were to have on her entire life. Raimond's philosophical convictions carried over into his notions of childrearing, and RB told of how he began his tutelage in sexual equality early:

In the same building where we lived was a school kept by M. Antin who was a Jansenist and who became a good friend of ours, my father showing this early a tendency to break with established things in spiritual matters, a tendency which grew with the years and which always left its stamp on me. Old Father Antin, as we called him reverentially, remarking that I was unoccupied, proposed to my father to take me as a pupil. So I entered the little

Raimond Bonheur: *Sophie Bonheur at Thirty-five*. Drawing, 1832. Klumpke. ❧ "She gave piano lessons, but hardly earned enough to keep hunger from the door of our home," Rosa reported bitterly to her friend Anna Klumpke of her mother's struggles to support the family in Paris. "My mother died from exhaustion after nursing me during my illness with scarlet fever. Her remains were buried in potter's field."

boys' class with my brothers, Auguste and Isidore. This was, I believe, the first pronounced step in a course which my father always pursued with us children and which in modern times has been named co-education. It emancipated me before I knew what emancipation meant and left me free to develop naturally and untrammeled. . . . I was generally a leader in all the games, and I did not hesitate now and again to use my fists. So from the very start, a masculine bent was given to my existence. . . .

The next few years of RB's life were filled with turbulence, often inspired by historical events. Since Raimond was so deeply engaged in political movements, the effect of each upheaval in France's unstable political life was immediately felt in the family circle. In 1830, incensed by Charles X's brazen repudiation of democratic principles, the people of Paris took to the barricades. RB was only eight when she witnessed the so-called "glorious days"—the three days of revolution leading to the ascension of Louis-Philippe—and she remembered them largely because her sister, Juliette, was born while the "cannons of the July revolution were thundering."

I do not exaggerate in employing this expression, for in front of our door a piece of artillery had been stationed which opened fire on the Place de Bastille not far away. Indeed I had a narrow escape from being a victim. My father had climbed on to the big street entrance door of our house so as to get a better view of the cannonade operations, and at the first discharge the door was so shaken that he fell off close by me. I recollect very well the charge of the royal guard, the shouts of the victorious combatants who drove them back. . . .

After the July revolution, Raimond had serious problems getting enough lessons to keep the family solvent. He was also increasingly preoccupied with his Saint-Simonianism. It was during this period that RB began to become aware of her mother's hard life. Things were made worse by the cholera epidemic of 1832, during which poor, terrified families such as the Bonheurs could do nothing but remain indoors hoping that some miracle would spare them. RB remembers peering from the window at the deserted streets where only carts filled with corpses would be seen. In his memoirs Dumas Père reports that

Honoré Daumier: *The Past—the Present—the Future.* Engraving, 1834. Print Collection, New York Public Library. ✿ This stinging caricature of Louis-Philippe was one of a series that Daumier made of the king who had been so swift to betray the ideals of his ardent and liberal supporters by becoming the unpardonable—a philistine. Daumier, Phillipon, and other satirists used a pear as a metaphor to escape censorship, but even so the vigilant police soon descended on the weekly journal *La Caricature* and forced a momentary pause in their protests.

for weeks the theaters were empty; only once did the actors have to play, and that was for an audience of one.

A year later, after nursing RB through an illness, Sophie fell ill herself and died. Raimond was faced with the problem of three motherless children, the oldest of whom, Rosa, was only eleven years old. His first move was to place the children as boarders with a friend of his sister, but after a few months he found a new apartment and took them all back to live with him. RB's next few years reflect her father's restlessness and his uncertainty. At first he tried to educate her in a trade, apprenticing her to a dressmaker. In later years she made a point of her distaste for such a feminine occupation, saying that she used to spend more time in the shop of the husband who made percus-

Rosa Bonheur: Sketch of a horse's head. 1835. Klumpke.
❧ This drawing was made when she was thirteen years old.

sion caps for fowling pieces than she did in the woman's atelier. Her father then put her with his friends M. and Mme. Bisson, who colored ceramic plates, engravings, and kaleidoscopic views. This suited RB better, and she made her first pennies in the arts with this odd couple. Mme. Bisson was, according to Rosa, an "original" who, disappointed at having no girls, rebaptized her three sons with girls' names.

Despite his daughter's relative contentment with the Bissons, Raimond began to feel that she needed a proper education and, when he was in a better financial position, he sent her to a real school. This led to disaster, as Rosa later attested with considerable relish:

I was sent to a boarding school kept by Mme. Gibert in the rue de Reuilly. Here I became an element of discord. My tomboy manners had an unfortunate influence on my companions, who soon grew turbulent. One day I proposed as a game a sham fight in the garden. We procured some wooden sabers and I ordered a cavalry charge. The result was the destruction of Mme. Gibert's fine rosebed which was her pride. This exploit was the last hair on the camel's back. The Giberts refused to harbor any longer such a noisy creature as I and sent me back home in disgrace.

(The sword brandished by RB was her recently acquired Templier souvenir.)

Whenever RB reminisced about her early years, she always stressed her mischievousness, her boyishness, and her native rebelliousness. Undoubtedly Raimond encouraged her and took pride in the unorthodox manner of upbringing that inspired such behavior. He gave way easily in the face of RB's unwillingness to be disciplined in school and made up his mind to train her to be a painter who would fulfill his Saint-Simonian ideals. After the fiasco of Mme. Gibert's school, Raimond took over her education at home. He allowed her to stay in the studio from the time she was thirteen. Each morning he gave her a task. Sometimes it was a plaster cast to copy, sometimes an engraving, and sometimes a still life. For some months he kept her to the academic system, working with pencils only. But one day, while he was out, RB attempted to paint a still life of cherries. When he returned he examined the study, praised her warmly, and then

began to encourage her to work from nature and to study land-scape, animals, and birds.

In 1836, at fourteen, RB was sent by her father to the Louvre to begin her real training in painting and sculpture. Although other young women used the Louvre as a school, being discrim-inated against in the academies, RB was one of the youngest and drew a great deal of attention. The attendants noticed her be-cause of her odd manner of dress and called her "the little Hus-sar." The older students, the *rapins*, noticed her because of her extreme youth and began by making fun of her. Later, she man-aged to win at least their tolerance and made amusing carica-tures of them in her leisure moments. She generally spent the whole day there, lunching on bread, a penny's worth of fried potatoes, and a mug of water taken from the fountain in the

(ABOVE LEFT) Rosa Bonheur: *Mon Professeur de Danse.* Watercolor, ca. 1837. Klumpke. ❦ From the mood of this sketch, we can infer that Rosa's dancing lessons were short-lived, as were most of her other studies.

(ABOVE RIGHT) Rosa Bonheur: Caricature of *rapin* at the Lou-vre. 1836. Klumpke. ❦ "... I went to study at the Louvre, where owing to my dress and manners, the guards gave me the name of '*le petit hussard*.' "

This is Rosa's playful inter-pretation of a young copyist— *un rapin*—at work there.

Rosa at sixteen. 1838. Klumpke. ❧ Throughout her life, Rosa was to make a habit of dressing up for photographs. She poses here as a proper young schoolgirl although in fact, garbed in boyish clothes, she mostly spent her days sketching barnyard animals in the outlying farms of Paris.

Louvre courtyard. Among works she mentions having copied are Porbus's *Henri IV*, which she sold immediately, Poussin's *Shepherds in Arcadia*, and Léopold Robert's *The Reapers*. In addition to studying paintings, she spent time in the sculpture gallery drawing from ancient casts.

She was in every way her father's pupil, following his instructions in her daily routine and taking his criticism in the evening. His anxiety about her formal education was apparent, and in the early years of her training he made her read the history of France after dinner. As her younger brothers grew into their teens, they joined RB, taking their initial training in the same way under the tutelage of Raimond (who had now begun to spell his name Raymond). The little family seemed to have formed a strong unit, quite independent of outside resources, and RB's memoirs abound in harmonious scenes of everybody drawing and painting. She rarely mentions any of Raymond's artist friends, or any of the artistic events that were shaping the newer trends in Paris.

From around 1836 to 1841, when she exhibited her first works in the annual Salon, RB gathered her notions of art almost entirely from Raymond. Some ideas may have been passed on to her from the friendlier young art students at the Louvre, but her father's authority remained paramount. Although there is little evidence that Raymond ever lost his horror of the romantic painters, he does appear to have modified his views during the later 1830s, by which time he had become head of a drawing school. He wrote to Lacour that when he took over the school it suffered from puerility due to its extreme concern with "finish" and its dependence on engravings instead of observations of nature. This typically romantic attack on "finish" as a deadening force is also reflected in his late remarks on drawing, although he still looked upon the painting techniques that flourished during the reign of Louis-Philippe as dangerously free.

5.
Science, Philosophy, and a Giraffe

At the time of the revolution resulting in the installation of Louis-Philippe as "King of the French," Raymond Bonheur, then in his thirties, was in the throes of his most exalted episode as a disciple. His Saint-Simonianism preoccupied him completely and strongly colored his view of the function of an artist. Basic to the Saint-Simonian doctrine was the rejection of what was repeatedly called "individualist" or "egoistic" art in favor of an art that would enlighten and instruct the masses. The romantic movement was considered dangerously out of touch with the demands of modern life, while the neoclassic approach was condemned as having little to do with the exigencies of the new industrial society. In his ardent way, Raymond clung to certain of the Saint-Simonian basic principles, but during the early years of the July monarchy he seemed to have been reconciled to Louis-Philippe's *juste-milieu* policies. The Saint-Simonians were not averse to the blandishments that Louis-Philippe offered artists in the early years of the regime, since he was favorably regarded as a king of industry, and it was during his tenure that some of the vast industrial schemes of Saint-Simon were undertaken, among them the network of railroads. The "bourgeois king" was not anathema to the Saint-Simonians as he was to the other socialist sects, thanks to his enterprising approach to communications.

The situation in the visual arts when Louis-Philippe took over was an impasse. The old quarrel, going back to the seventeenth century when the Poussinists raged against the Rubensists, had finally waned. The classicists and the romantics no longer seemed irreconcilable to the new students, who could see merits on both sides. From their ranks emerged a group of "independents" who detached themselves from partisan quarrels and went off in search of neutral territory. A new species of genre and landscape painter appeared, indifferent to the ancient theoretical disputes and eager to take inspiration directly from nature. Among them were Théodore Rousseau, Camille Corot, and Narcisse-Vergile Diaz, all of whom gained entry into the official art world through the first annual Salon established by Louis-Philippe.

By the mid-1830s, the *juste-milieu* policy of the government had made headway in the art world, and many artists were being supported by government patronage. They took care not to veer too far in any direction, for their status under the July monarchy depended on their discretion. Such status conferred on them the opportunity to earn a living from numerous government commissions (mostly to make copies of works approved by the government) and to gain a larger and larger bourgeois audience through exposure in the Salons and through the King's well-publicized attention. Baudelaire referred to these artists as "amiable eclectics" and in 1845, writing about Léon Cogniet (who had once written the young RB a flattering letter), he summed up the traits that characterized the most visible artists since 1830:

> If he does not aspire to the level of genius, he is one of those talents which defy criticism by their very completeness within their own moderation. M. Cogniet is as unacquainted with the reckless flights of fantasy as with the rigid systems of the absolutists. To fuse, to mix and combine, while exercising choice, have always been his role and aim; and he has perfectly fulfilled them.

Professor Albert Boime cites an unsigned article in the journal *L'Artiste* characterizing the Salon of 1831 as the artistic epitome of the *juste-milieu* movement:

> Conscientious drawing, but not of the Jansenistic kind practiced by Ingres; the effect, but without everything having been sacrificed in its behalf; color, but which will approximate as closely as

L'Abbé Lamennais: *Paroles d'un Croyant.* Atelier, By. ❧ "He defined everything I searched for," said Rosa of the writings of the revolutionary theologian-philosopher Felicité de Lamennais. His book *Paroles d'un Croyant* was always near at hand.

possible the tones of nature, and not result from bizarre tones veiling the real with the fantastic; poetry, but which will not need hell, tombs, and dreams as its necessary complement, nor yet replace the ideal with the ugly: here is what distinguishes the school which I will designate as "the transition."

Much of the artistic rhetoric of the 1830s serves only to cover up a basic confusion in the goals and ideals of artists within the new monarchical structure. Raymond Bonheur evidently supplemented his Saint-Simonian principles with writings by romantic radicals such as Pierre Leroux and the Abbé Lammenais, while yet assimilating the new mild temper of the times. He especially commended Lammenais to his children. RB told Léon Roger-Milès, "My father made me read Lammenais, and Lammenais defined everything that I have sought."

Just what the erstwhile priest and Catholic reformer actually defined remains vague, as were the Abbé's writings in general. But RB clung tenaciously to his pieties and often quoted them to friends. The Abbé had started life as a conservative priest but had been converted to the radical principles of free association—the prototype of collective bargaining—and universal suffrage. Fired by the revolution of 1830, Lammenais founded an important newspaper, *L'Avenir*, together with Charles Montalembert, in which he sketched the philosophy he would later publish in book form. Basically, this former priest advocated a romantic Christianity which he called "universal brotherhood" and which would be safeguarded by universal suffrage. He examined the position of the modern worker and stated in 1839 that it was the same as that of ancient slaves and medieval serfs. Since Christianity posits that all men have equal rights, the Abbé argued, a republican form of government with a socialist philosophy was the only proper Christian solution.

Lammenais's quirky personality had attracted George Sand, who for several years tried to move him from a "position of prophet and apocalyptic poet" to one of political leader, but he resisted (although he did not resist her material support for his newspapers and pamphlets). She wrote, "Those who came across him for the first time when he was in one of his brooding fits, and saw no more than a greenish, rather wild eye and a great nose edged like a sword, were apt to take fright and say that his appearance was positively devilish." But his controversial articles and books, among them *Paroles d'un Croyant*, which got him excommunicated, and *Le Pays et le Gouvernement*, which earned him a year in Louis-Philippe's prisons, were widely read.

L'Abbé Lammenais's radical Christian politics and his idealistic aesthetics undoubtedly appealed to Raymond. During 1830 and 1831 there were many columns addressed to artists in *L'Avenir*, always calling for the abolition of the "egoistic individualism" associated with romanticism. In his *Sketch for a Philosophy* (1840) Lammenais restated the principles he had vigorously promulgated in *L'Avenir:*

> Art is nothing but the exterior form of ideas, the expression of religious dogma and the social principles dominant in certain epochs.... Art loses itself when the artist no longer has faith in the conception to which his works are linked, or when his works are not linked to any conception.

Lammenais thought artists should not imitate ancient art, not even their immediate predecessors. But, on the other hand, he said that artists should not try to reproduce nature, since purely descriptive art is decadent:

> Life and art must be sought not in the past, which cannot be reborn, but in that which is germinating in the soul of the present. Today's artists, the real artists, have only two ways to go. They can, closing themselves in, individualize art, thus expressing themselves only. But what is a man in humanity? To isolate oneself from the beginning is to renounce great inspirations, to forsake the idea of awaking general and deep sympathies, of speaking a universally understood language.... Artists can, by descending into the bowels of society, recapture in themselves the palpitating life which they can inject into their works, and which animates their work as the spirit of God animates and fills the universe. The old world is dissolving ... the religion of the future projects its first rays on the human genre: *the artist must be its prophet.*

Although Lammenais's Platonic leanings seemed ill-adapted to the aggressive social theory he advocated, the Bonheur family, like many other people including George Sand, were exhilarated by them. Raymond seemed quite satisfied with the vague and often pietistic aesthetics that Lammenais put forward, and when RB spent time with her biographer Roger-Milès, she must have cited specific passages, such as:

> In the reproduction of natural forms, art must try to reproduce not the simple phenomenon, the pure sensible aspect of form, but the immaterial example, and this example constitutes for each determined form another order, an order secondary to the ideal Beauty whose splendor must radiate through the corporeal image, and which helps to rise toward absolute Beauty.

And:

> Nature, in the breast of which archetypes of beings are incarnated, presents only phenomena of corporeal forms, opaque envelopes of the invisible essence. Art is thus not a simple imitation of nature; it must reveal, under that which strikes the senses, the intense principle, the ideal beauty that only the spirit perceives and that God eternally contemplates. . . .

From the mid to late 1830s at least, Raymond was an assiduous reader of the local Christianizing radical prophets. He imbued his daughter with his warm but vague enthusiasm and in general held to the Lammenais formulas in his own work. Yet he encouraged Rosa to develop her skill in depicting aspects of nature on the spot, and he supported her growing interest in animals as her exclusive subject. In this he was probably influenced by the interest recently shown by the bourgeois public in animal representations by the painters Constant Troyon and Jacques Raymond Brascassat. Raymond may not have accepted romanticism, but he seemed to have fallen into a few fashionable romantic positions. For instance, under Raymond's guidance RB was reading, like the *rapins* she met in the Louvre, both Sir Walter Scott and Ossian. During the evening sketching sessions at home, Raymond often read aloud to his children, choosing works that were commonly appreciated by the romantic generation, though *not* Victor Hugo. Raymond also taught her, with Saint-Simonian reverence, the power and importance of modern science. She made a point of reading popular scientific authors and in later years acquired a number of scientific books describing recent progress. Sometimes she tartly reminded her admirers that she was no sentimentalist but followed objective scientific methods. In this she was faithful to her father's insistence that religion must defer to science.

Although Raymond had adjusted his views in the 1830s to correspond more nearly to the program of the period—the romanticism that led painters to abandon history painting in favor of nature—a fortuitous encounter was to greatly advance his interest in science. In his struggle to maintain his family Raymond had been obliged to seek free-lance work in addition to his drawing lessons. His old friends the Silvelas once again helped him by introducing him to France's best-known scientist, Etienne Geoffroy de Saint-Hilaire, who eventually, probably in 1833 or 1834, engaged Raymond to do a large number of illustrations for his work at the zoological gardens. Raymond became a close friend of the Saint-Hilaire family, and RB remained in close touch with them all her life.

RB's views on the art of portraying animals were strongly influenced by the prevailing trends in natural history. Since the days of Diderot and the *philosophes*, French intellectuals had evinced exceptional interest in natural history. During the revolutionary period the government had authorized the founding of a museum of natural history and the zoological garden, to both of which Saint-Hilaire had been appointed professor. In 1798 he had joined a group of scholars and artists on a junket with Napoleon to Egypt, where he remained for four years amassing a remarkable collection of objects for study ranging from ancient fossils to mummies for the new French museums. This early period in Egypt led to his greatest exploit years later when he was sent on a mission to import Europe's first giraffe for the zoo. His triumphant return to Europe was a public event, and he became as well known to the French public as any politician or theatrical personality.

Although fifty-five years old and in poor health, Saint-Hilaire undertook to see the giraffe safely to Paris from the port of Marseilles. After studying the problem carefully, he decided that the only way to traverse France would be to bring the animal on

(LEFT) *The Giraffe.* Lithograph, ca. 1835. ✿ Soon after her arrival in Paris during the summer of 1827, the giraffe that Geoffroy de Saint-Hilaire had dramatically escorted from Marseilles was stabled in a beautiful rotunda in the Jardin des Plantes, which had been designed and built to fit her elegant greatness. "The crowds who go to see *La Fille d'Abyssinie* are delirious," reported an observer for *L'Illustration.* "The devotion she has for her constant companions—two cows who also made the long voyage from the East with her—is touching."

(RIGHT) The Comparative Anatomy Collection at the Jardin des Plantes. Lithograph, ca. 1845. ✿ The scientific and philosophic speculations of Buffon, Saint-Hilaire, and Cuvier seized the fancy of the Parisian public of the 1840s. A visit to the Jardin des Plantes to see the strange "new" skeletons there became a popular Sunday pastime.

---

foot in small stages. He designed an impermeable gummed-rubber cape for the giraffe's body and a hood with wings that reached its chest to protect it from inclement weather. In addition to the giraffe, Etienne had brought an antelope, two wild sheep from Corsica, and a few other unspecified animals. On May 20, 1827, the caravan left Marseilles, and the trip was estimated at fifty-two days. Two mounted gendarmes rode ahead to stop traffic, followed by a brigadier, three more mounted gen-

---

darmes, and three cows, after which came Saint-Hilaire himself with the giraffe and six attendants. Every newspaper in France recorded the daily progress of the bizarre procession. By the time it reached Paris, hordes of people had ridden out twenty miles to greet them, among them the younger scientist Georges Léopold Cuvier and the author Stendhal. The King and the Duchesse de Berri had wanted to meet the giraffe en route, but Mme. La Dauphine decreed that it was up to the giraffe to come to the King. And so, on the 30th of June, 1827, the whole caravan had to go for a royal audience to Saint-Cloud.

If the French populace knew Etienne Geoffroy de Saint-Hilaire through the colorful story of the giraffe's arrival in Paris, Raymond and his friends were much more excited by the great debate between Etienne and his former protégé, Cuvier, which took place from February to April in 1830 at the Royal Academy of Sciences. This long debate had been brewing ever since Etienne had returned from Egypt, and when it finally occurred in public it was front-page news for more than two months. Correspondents from all over Europe attended, and interest in natural history was enormously stimulated by their emotional reports as the journalists took sides and wrote passionately on behalf of one or the other contender. (An example of the importance of these debates is cited by Goethe's disciple Eckermann

Georges Cuvier: *Le Règne Animal.* Atelier, By. ⚜ "One must know what is under their skin," Rosa said. "Otherwise your animal will look like a mat rather than a tiger."

Her mentors were the illustrious naturalist and author Etienne Geoffroy de Saint-Hilaire, a friend of her father, and Georges Cuvier, a pioneer in the field of comparative anatomy.

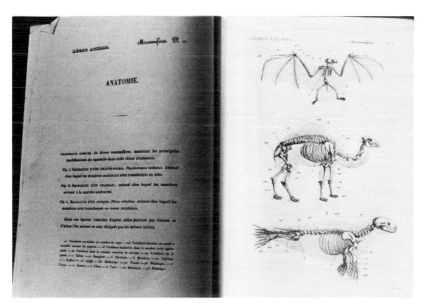

Pierre-Jean David d'Angers: *Georges Cuvier*. Engraving of the statue, 1835. American Museum of Natural History, New York. ⚜ A statue of the French paleontologist and pioneer of comparative anatomy made by the noted medalist David d'Angers was erected in Montbeliard, Cuvier's native city, three years after his death.

who had visited Goethe to speak of the momentous news of the 1830 revolution. Goethe greeted him at the door saying, "Well, what do you think of the great event? The volcano has erupted; everything is in flames. From now on it is no longer a debate behind closed doors." Eckermann, thinking Goethe referred to the revolution, spoke of the deposition of Charles X, but Goethe interrupted impatiently, "I don't speak of those people. I'm speaking of the debate between Cuvier and Geoffroy de Saint-Hilaire.")

Saint-Hilaire's theories about the relationships among all living beings were based on the philosophical principle that in nature there is a "unity of composition." His supporters agreed, and, as one of them reported, "Today, science pursues other ends than in the past. Then it was a question of founding zoology. Now we seek a knowledge of the philosophic resemblance of things." Saint-Hilaire's motto in Latin, *Ab uno disce omnes* ("Out of one come all"), roused the ire of the younger Cuvier, who was a passionate opponent of the popular notion of analogy (now called homology).

In his published account of the debates, Saint-Hilaire reports that they began on February 15 when he presented a paper by two younger scientists that proved the validity of his own theory of a single pattern for all animals, a "unity of plan and composition." They had compared anatomical structures of cephalopods such as squid, octopus, and cuttlefish with a variety of vertebrates, and found definite similarities. Two years later the physicist André-Marie Ampère further supported Saint-Hilaire's theory by stating that "when an animal changes its condition of existence, all that is essential to its organism subsists while new formations appear in relation to the new environment."

Essentially, Etienne Geoffroy de Saint-Hilaire's theory was an attack on the Aristotelian descriptive method, which had dominated the natural sciences up to the 1830s. "The ancient method," he said, "stops in its applications just at that point where it should have become a doctrine, where it should have become an Ariadne's thread in order to make apparent the most hidden rapports, the common points of general facts." Saint-Hilaire felt that pure description of facts was not enough, but that facts should be employed principally in order to establish relationships. Since the objectives of zoology had changed, the most important task for the zoologist would be to describe the philosophic resemblance of beings. "Animals," he wrote, "are the product of a single system of composition, which I have called the unity of organic compositions." The mere study of form and function could never reveal a philosophy—only Saint-Hilaire's own method of comparative anatomy could do that. Forms and functions may differ, but the basic components and their connections do not differ from species to species.

Saint-Hilaire's emphasis on the principle of analogy found a warm response in the literary and artistic community, that was already accustomed to the notion of romantic organicism. Goethe had written earlier, "All nature's children must have been modeled upon one basic pattern, which might be called the prototype," and "individuality is always a metamorphic variation of an original type or interindividual pattern." The great rhyming scheme of all things under creation had also preoccupied French and British poets from Coleridge to Baudelaire during the first half of the nineteenth century. Such views proved to be consoling in the struggle against what artists perceived to be a pernicious, growing materialism in modern life. Geoffroy de Saint-Hilaire became a hero to all those who watched the rise of industrialism with mixed feelings and were happy to see the mechanistic interpretation of existence challenged. He also fed into the Darwinian tendency of the later part of the century, in which such artists as Rosa Bonheur could easily elaborate on theories of animal relationships without embarrassment. Saint-Hilaire's ideas enabled RB to relate the animal world to the human and served as a foundation for her vision of her role as an artist.

Pierre-Jean David d'Angers: *Etienne Geoffroy de Saint-Hilaire.* Engraving of a bronze medallion, 1831. American Museum of Natural History, New York. ❧ A friend of RB's father, this illustrious nineteenth-century naturalist was the author of the controversial work *Philosophie Anatomique,* which was to fire the famous Cuvier–Saint-Hilaire debates at the Royal Academy of Science in 1830.

Rosa Bonheur: *Shepherd and His Sheep*. Oil, 1841. Klumpke. ❧ This was painted at a time when the young Bonheur clan kept a veritable menagerie in their cramped studio in Paris. Their pet sheep, which Auguste would carry down five flights of stairs to graze on the Monçeau Plain, might have been one of the models for this pastoral scene.

6.
First Success

All through her teens RB was attentive to her father's admonitions. His Saint-Simonian suspicion of "individualistic" art and his theories of natural history were powerful elements in her training, in which the direct observation of nature was stressed. While she spent hours in the Louvre copying (mostly the Dutch masters Paulus Potter, Wouvermans, and Van Berghem), she also worked in the communal family studio, studying the structures of objects, various animals, and birds. In all the accounts of RB's life covering the period before her first participation in the Salon of 1841, there are no references to contemporary events in the art world and almost none to the major painters of the day. The old masters in the Louvre and her apprenticeship to Raymond were her chief sources of stimulation. The family circle did include a few of Raymond's old friends from Bordeaux and a few of his patrons, but the sophisticated world of contemporary art always seemed alien and suspicious to him and his children. RB's formation as an artist was therefore relatively uncomplicated and only minimally affected by the urbane artistic culture of modern Paris.

Raymond's frequent changes in domicile did not seem to disturb the working pattern of family life. When Rosa's brothers, Isidore and Auguste, and her sister, Juliette, were old enough, they joined her in her father's studio, where they were assigned the same daily tasks as their sister had been given. In the evenings there were drawing sessions while someone read aloud.

The studio, in which each member of the family occupied his habitual place, was

a confusion of all sorts of odds and ends, and you would never guess how my father took advantage of that disorder. When he received money for his work he would take a handful and throw it at random about the room, and then, when we had not a penny at home, we searched all corners of the room, sometimes finding a five-franc piece which saved us from starvation.

Raymond took an indulgent attitude toward his daughter's growing predilection for animals and allowed her to establish a small menagerie at home. In 1841 when he took quarters in the rue Rumford, the nineteen-year-old Rosa was keeping rabbits, chickens, ducks, quails, canaries, finches, and a goat there. Raymond also encouraged Rosa's decision to be an animal painter and urged her to study her subjects from every point of view. In her later teens she frequented a farm in the village of Villiers, where she sometimes lodged for days at a time with a peasant woman. There she studied animals in their natural environment and even undertook to dissect them, seeking to improve her knowledge of anatomy, osteology, and myology, as Raymond had done under the patronage of Geoffroy de Saint-Hilaire.

In spite of the obvious pressures of poverty, Rosa did in later years recall her adolescence as a period relatively free of conflict. She cheerfully developed her skills and maintained a boyish camaraderie with her father and younger brothers that seemed to satisfy her social needs. The remarriage of Raymond in 1842 to Marguerite Picard Peyrol, a 29-year-old widow, was undoubtedly significant in bringing a new sense of stability and comfort to the Bonheur household. The Bonheur children affectionately called Marguerite "Mamiche," and her presence brought young Rosa the gift of freedom, for no longer was she needed to help care for her younger brothers and sisters. Her stepbrother, Hippolyte Peyrol, described the family's tranquil working days and the games in the early evenings in which RB took part:

Sometimes she played horse with Isidore. She would put a big drawing pencil in his mouth as a bit with a cord attached to either

Rosa Bonheur: *Birds in the Studio.* Drawing, 1841. Klumpke. ❧ Raymond Bonheur (he now spelled his first name with a *y*) once wrote to Rosa, who was away for a few days, "The canaries are singing the 'Gloria Tibi, Domine' and the finch is getting steadier on its legs. The rats are off wandering somewhere or other."

end, and thus harnessed, horse and driver would go rushing wildly over the Monçeau Plain and finally return home covered with dust and in a dripping perspiration.

The only evidence of Rosa's having a close relationship with anyone outside the family was her friendship with Nathalie Micas, which began when RB was fourteen. Nathalie had been Raymond's pupil some years before, and in her late reminiscences, RB describes her first meeting with Nathalie sometime around 1830, when the Bonheur family had moved into a gloomy stone house whose concierge made children's toys. He used to buy the skins for the shuttlecocks from a Mme. Micas, who had a little girl. "We used to come across the poor, pale-looking child often with her comical hat that made us laugh, with a green eyeshade over her eyes to protect them. All the pupils of M. Antin's school were just at the age, as La Fontaine says, that knows no pity. We made fun of her on account of her weak, sickly air."

Nathalie's sickliness made her father anxious, and in 1836, when she was twelve, he commissioned Raymond to paint her portrait, as he did not expect her to survive very long. RB was introduced to the Micas household and immediately attached Nathalie to herself as friend and dependent. Nathalie needed the stronger child as protector and in return busied herself with motherly chores that RB never found easy, such as keeping her clothes in good repair, sewing, and looking after the studio. This friendship, which RB often characterized as "sisterly," lasted

Rosa Bonheur: *Nathalie Micas.*
Watercolor, ca. 1850. Klumpke.
⚜ This small portrait was
made soon after Bonheur left her
family home on the rue Rumford. "With my father dead,
there was no one left at home to
share my joys and my sorrows,"
Bonheur told one of her biographers, "so I went to live with
the Micases and from then on I
considered Nathalie my sister."

until Nathalie's death in 1889. Although it was never openly ac-
knowledged as a love relationship, RB always tended to be am-
biguous on the subject, telling her friends that she had not had
time for marriage, or that painting was her sole passion, or that
no one had ever loved her enough to marry her.

In the beginning the friendship with Nathalie was doubly
welcome to RB, who had sorely missed being mothered in the
rue Rumford household. At the Micas home both mother and father were only too happy to include Rosa in the family circle
because of her protective attitude toward their daughter. The
extent of their need for her is indicated by the bizarre account of
the deathbed scene of father Micas in 1848. He summoned the

two young women and admonished them to stay together, giving them his blessing as if they were about to marry.

With Nathalie and the daily routine in the Bonheur family circle as stabilizing influences, RB could pursue her ambition to be an animal painter with undivided attention. In 1840 at the age of nineteen she had succeeded in placing two works in the annual Salon which reflected Louis-Philippe's *juste-milieu* philosophy rather faithfully. Her painting *Rabbits Nibbling Carrots* and a drawing of some goats and sheep were hung, although not commented upon by critics or judges. Still, Raymond was justifiably proud. The following year, and every year until 1855, RB exhibited her landscapes and animal studies in the annual Salons, in which the "amiable eclectics" were very successful. The style of these works seems to have been influenced somewhat by the Barbizon school, a group of landscapists who abandoned both romantic and classic canons in favor of natural observation. These artists, including Théodore Rousseau and Camille Corot, had been influenced in turn by Dutch landscape painters and had found an eager audience.

In 1842 RB sent four works, including *Evening Falling Over a Ploughed Field, Cow Lying in a Field, Horse for Sale,* and a sculpture of a reclining ewe, which one critic compared favorably with the major animal sculptor of the period, Antoine-Louis Barye. Barye's direct studies in the Jardin des Plantes from 1823 to 1831 had led him to the innovative romantic style of rendering animals in active poses and earned him a unique position among sculptors of his time.

After RB had exhibited for three years in the Salons, she began to sell her works regularly. With what remained of the profits after she contributed to the household expenses, she began to travel in the countryside. She studied different breeds of cows, bulls, and sheep. Her first official acknowledgment came in the Salon of 1845, to which she sent six works, when she was awarded a third-class medal. For the first time her work caught the attention of one of the important critics, Théophile Thoré, who noted that her bulls were worth more than those of the popular animal painter J-R. Brascassat. The occasion was one of great rejoicing for the Bonheur family, all of whom regarded official success as the highest goal. In 1845, however,

(ABOVE) Rosa Bonheur: *Rabbits Nibbling Carrots*. Oil, 1840. Musée des Beaux-Arts, Bordeaux (54 × 65 cm). ❧ Painted when she was eighteen, this little scene of two rabbits nibbling on carrots and a turnip was Rosa's entry to the Salon of 1841. The critics accepted it with silence.

(RIGHT) Rosa Bonheur: *Mallard Ducks*. Ink, ca. 1846. Klumpke.

"there was no solemn distribution of medals as there is today," RB recalled late in life. "The laureates had to go and fetch them in the office of the director. My father, who wanted to accustom me to not count on anyone but myself, sent me all alone. I went with all the courage of my twenty-three years, presenting myself before the director of the Beaux-Arts, who handed me the medal, complimenting me in the name of the King. You can imagine his stupefaction when I responded, 'Thank the King for me and be kind enough to add that I will try to do better another time.'"

In the next Salon she did do better, this time drawing a few more lines from Thoré, a vigorous and widely respected critic already known for his intelligent support of the independent landscapists. Later he would become a champion of Millet and Courbet, with whom, at least initially, he associated Rosa Bonheur. Her flock of sheep, he said, made one wish to become a shepherd with a crook, silk vest, and ribbons. A year later, in 1847, he again wrote of her:

> Mlle. Rosa Bonheur, who, before the French revolution, would have been a member of the Academy of Fine Arts, has brought oxen under the yoke and has her sheep rest in the meadows of Cantal. Mlle. Rosa paints almost like a man. What a pity her strong brush is not held also by M. Verboeckenhoven and the other *précieux* who paint like young ladies.

If Thoré was only mildly complimentary, another critic, Anatole de LaForge, was ecstatic about the "courageous young girl" who had braved the storms of the art world to produce her cows "that have the air of being good mothers of a family." Unfortunately, his 1856 book, *Contemporary Painting in France*, in which he wrote at length about RB, is somewhat diminished by his mediocre preferences. Pointing out that George Sand called Delacroix the most important painter of this period, he begs to differ, saying that "Delacroix is not the most important painter in a country which counts names like those of Ingres, Ary Scheffer, and Paul Delaroche. He is their emulator, that's all one can say."

7.
The Question of Sex

During the mid-1840s, RB began to frequent the slaughter-houses of Paris, following a tradition established by an artist she had come to admire, Théodore Géricault. Not surprisingly, her presence caused consternation among the slaughterhouse workers, who were baffled by this small, boyish young woman with her cropped hair and quick stride, her slightly lowered head, and her bold, determined glance. Rosa Bonheur was well aware of the effect she created:

> To perfect myself in the study of nature I spent whole days in the Roule slaughterhouse. One must be greatly devoted to art to stand the sight of such horrors, in the midst of the coarsest people. They wondered at seeing a young woman taking interest in their work and made themselves as disagreeable to me as they possibly could. But when our aims are right, we always find help. Providence sent me a protector in the good Monsieur Emile, a butcher of great physical strength. He declared that whoever fails to be polite to me would have to reckon with him. I was thus enabled to work undisturbed.

Not only did M. Emile protect RB, but he also bought her sketches and arranged for others, including a wholesale grocer and a wholesale shirtmaker, to follow suit. RB was still young and open enough for those she encountered to be startled, amused, and protective. She was an appealing figure, and her early success was certainly partially due to her personality. Even with her bold manners, men found her endearing, and not a few of her colleagues took a protective stance similar to M. Emile's in her early career.

RB's use of masculine attire is said to have begun during this period when conventional women's clothing would have been inconvenient, although some historians report that she began to wear trousers and mannish blouses later on while preparing *The Horse Fair*, which required her to visit the horse markets. Whatever the case, RB did begin to flout convention in her twenties in the open manner that had already made George Sand notorious. RB, however, was never as provocative as Sand. She insisted that she wore men's clothing only for work and then only for practical purposes. There is good reason to believe that she vacillated between middle-class modesty and bohemian audacity all her life. Raymond's Saint-Simonian feminism obviously affected her life, but RB seems never to have been completely comfortable as a rebel against society. Her own feminism often faltered, reflecting the duplicity that had been inherent in French attitudes ever since the French Revolution.

Despite the professed sympathy of the eighteenth-century revolutionaries for the injustices endured by women, many of the most celebrated leaders had harbored invincible prejudices. Their successor, Napoleon, shared their reservations, and when the Code Napoléon was drafted, most of the revolutionary ideals were abandoned, for which lapse feminists of the period blamed the popularity of Rousseau's *Emile*. Any touch of eccentricity, or any suggestion of lesbianism, was resented and sometimes unmercifully criticized. Alexandre Dumas Père, writing of Mlle. Raucourt, a Napoleonic tragedienne, ironically commented:

> Mlle. Raucourt's feeling toward men passed beyond indifference and amounted to hatred. Yet, strangely enough, when the costume of her sex did not demand it, she wore that of our sex. Very often she gave lessons to her lovely pupil in trousers, usually with a pretty young woman present who addressed her as "my dear fellow" and a charming child who called her "papa."

Even after the 1830 revolution, intellectuals and artists were loath to admit the equality they felt obliged to grant women in principle. They were particularly irritated by those women who, encouraged by George Sand's example, tried to penetrate

(LEFT) Alcide Lorentz: *George Sand*. Drawing, 1842. Bibliothèque Nationale, Paris. ❧ Like Rosa, George Sand was ridiculed for wearing male attire.

> "If this portrait of George Sand,
>   Leaves the spirit a bit perplexed,
>   It is that Genius is abstract,
>   And as we know has no sex."

(RIGHT) Maleuvre: *Young Saint-Simonian*. Engraving, 1832. ❧ This engraving represents the costume of *"la femme libre,"* the female member of the Saint-Simon movement. All through her life, Bonheur was to wear an unbelted and rugged version of this outfit, but only during work-time.

the professional world of the arts. Honoré Daumier, otherwise so liberal in his views, made three different series of prints poking fun at militant women, the most searing being his "Bluestocking" series, which included a picture of a thin, sharp-nosed lady novelist reading a newspaper in a restaurant, saying, "No review of my novel yet! These journalists take no notice of me. . . . It is inconceivable!" Another showed an exceptionally homely woman pointing to her portrait and saying, "The artist has depicted me in the act of writing my sad volume, *Vapors of My Soul.*" Daumier also attacked campaigning feminists and socialists in many drawings that show more than a little animus toward them. He paralleled Flaubert, whose caricature of a woman of letters, Mlle. Vatnaz, appeared in *L'Education Sentimentale.* Flaubert drew her as an ordinary schoolteacher from the provinces who struggles to act like a sophisticated Parisienne and who displays ridiculous ambitions and meager creative means. Flaubert could not have been more contemptuous, despite his valued friendship with George Sand.

Such resistance did not, however, deter the women who had been fired by the rhetoric of sympathetic socialist writers. RB's admiration for George Sand was her principal source of encouragement. Sand became the model for outwardly rebellious behavior, and her position was strengthened by the writings of other feminists, especially the sensational Flora Tristan. This eccentric, colorful grandmother of Paul Gauguin was far more outspoken than Sand herself, and in her *Emancipation of Women*, published posthumously in late 1845, she demanded rights that women even today have not fully achieved. Tristan's influence was deeply felt in the circles that the Bonheurs frequented, where her bold assertions were considered the most important statements ever made in the battle for women's rights.

All the same, RB never wholly embraced the theoretical program outlined by her father, and she frequently contradicted herself about the problems of feminism. On the matter of dress, for instance, she staunchly maintained that her donning of trousers and boots was only a matter of convenience. She always pointed out that her workman's blouses were embroidered and often ridiculed women who renounced their habitual dress in order to pass themselves off as men. "If you see me dressed as I am, it is not for originality's sake, as too many women do, but simply to facilitate my work." She even called attention to a residue of coquetry in her nature: "Despite the metamorphoses of my costume, there isn't a daughter of Eve who appreciates more than I the nuances. My brusque and even a bit primitive nature never impeded my heart from remaining perfectly feminine."

The American critic Henry Bacon, who frequented her studio in later years, reported that she never permitted a picture or a photograph to be made of her in masculine attire. One day he arrived too early and caught her in her working clothes. "Well," she said, "now that you've seen me, I need not change. But had I expected you so early you would have found me *en dame*."

RB maintained affectionate, comradely relationships of long duration with several men, among them a few painters, throughout her life. Yet there are numerous hints in her recorded conversations that she harbored deep resentments toward men. Her attitude was indelibly marked by the memory of her mother's tragedy, and through her mother's example she came to believe that women who marry are doomed always to a life of a "subaltern."

> The memory of the silent devotion of my mother reminds me that it is in the nature of men to manifest their opinions without preoccupying themselves with the impression they make on the spirit of their companions.

One of her rare direct statements of hostile suspicion is found among her marginal notes on the copy of the first published biography of her by Eugène de Mirecourt. The biography appeared in 1856, and she kept making corrections in the margins all her life:

> I have remarked that if a woman is not a little coquettish, she comes near to being a virago. If she is virtuous, and at the same time graceful, handsome, and kind, she is sure to have many admirers; and each of them through pique will try to blacken her reputation and to take advantage of her. While studying animals, I have, like Molière and La Fontaine, studied my human brothers just as they have studied their sisters.

SECRÉTARIAT GÉNÉRAL.
2e BUREAU.
No 212.
Signalement.
Taille: 1 m. 50
Âge de 35 ans
Cheveux châtains
Sourcils id
Front ordinaire
Yeux bruns
Nez ordinaire
Bouche moyenne
Menton rond
Visage ovale
Teint ordinaire
Signes particuliers:
Signature du porteur.

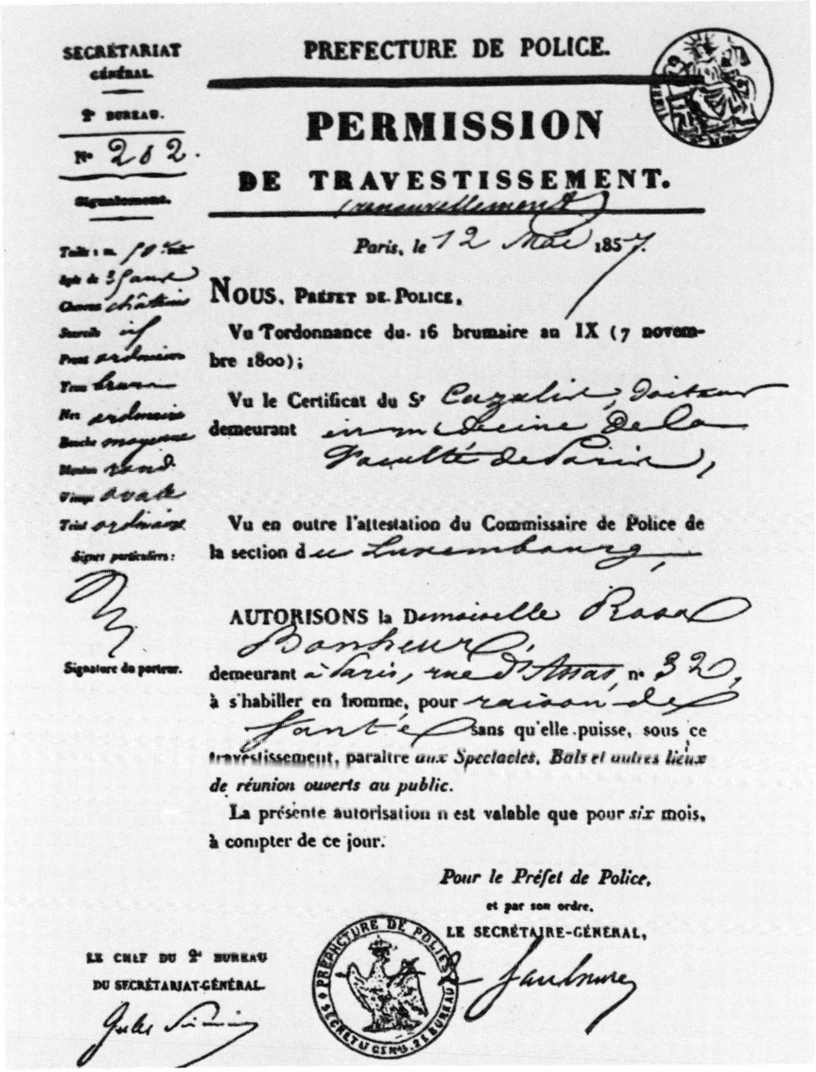

PREFECTURE DE POLICE.

PERMISSION

DE TRAVESTISSEMENT.

(renouvellement)

Paris, le 12 Mai 1857.

NOUS, PRÉFET DE POLICE,

Vu l'ordonnance du 16 brumaire an IX (7 novembre 1800);

Vu le Certificat du Sr Cazalis, docteur demeurant [illegible] de la Faculté de Paris;

Vu en outre l'attestation du Commissaire de Police de la section du Luxembourg,

AUTORISONS la Demoiselle Rosa Bonheur, demeurant à Paris, rue d'Assas, no 32, à s'habiller en homme, pour raison de santé sans qu'elle puisse, sous ce travestissement, paraître *aux Spectacles, Bals et autres lieux de réunion ouverts au public.*

La présente autorisation n'est valable que pour *six* mois, à compter de ce jour.

Pour le Préfet de Police,
et par son ordre,
LE SECRÉTAIRE-GÉNÉRAL,

LE CHEF DU 2e BUREAU
DU SECRÉTARIAT-GÉNÉRAL.

This is a copy of one of the police certificates issued to Rosa Bonheur giving her permission to wear male attire in public, with restrictions against attending "Spectacles, balls or other public meeting places" in such attire. Renewable every six months, the permit was given "for reasons of health" and was countersigned by her doctor.

Another straightforward statement of her disdain for men occurred when she had several women to lunch at her château at By. She wanted to offer a rare yucca plant to one of them and asked her gardener to dig it up, being careful not to cut the roots. When he returned he had, indeed, cut the roots, and RB remarked, "What do you think, ladies? Isn't that a beautiful example of male intelligence?"

EMANCIPATION DE LA FEMME.

SAPEURS. Vu ses nombreux services cette troupe tiendra la tête...

TAMBOUR. Spécialement destiné à rassembler la troupe et à battre la charge.

GARDE VILLAGEOISE. Qué qui va là?..

GRENADIER. Ce corps est affecté au service de nuit, qu'il fera avec la garde nationale.

The frankest avowal was reported by a male family friend:

After my marriage, when RB was riding out with me, but this time in lady's dress, we happened to meet a gentleman friend of mine. He remarked in fun, "Mme. Verdier is unwise to let you two ride out together. In her place I shouldn't be so tranquil." "Oh, yes, dear sir," replied Rosa Bonheur, "if you only knew how little I care for your sex, you wouldn't get such queer ideas into your head. The fact is, in the way of males, I like only the bulls I paint."

(OPPOSITE) Caricature of women's rights movement. Lithograph, ca. 1840. ⚜ The French Army is taken over by women in this spoof on the *femme libre* movement.

When France was invaded by the Prussians in 1870, Rosa quickly took up her rifle and volunteered to defend her village. The mayor was not pleased. "You are no Jeanne d'Arc," he told her firmly.

(RIGHT) *The Studio Smock*. Lithograph, ca. 1845 (artist unknown). ⚜ An adaptation of this classic *blouse d'atelier* worn by many male artists of the time was also chosen by RB as her daily painting costume. This might account for some of the colorful gossip that she dressed like a man.

8.
The End of Revolution

Rosa Bonheur was in her mid-twenties when Louis-Philippe's regime foundered dramatically. Her father enthusiastically welcomed the upheavals of February 1848, and RB saw herself for a time as a staunch republican at his side. Her favorite model, George Sand, who had earlier espoused Christian socialist principles, became caught up in the excitement of the February revolution and came forward in support of far more radical factions fighting for a socialist republic. "I am a Communist now," she wrote early in 1848, "much as I might have been a Christian in A.D. 50."

The early promise shown by Louis-Philippe, at least from a liberal point of view, was quickly dissipated after he became King. (Of course, Raymond, who had very early experienced the harshness of Louis-Philippe's repressive laws, was never taken in, nor were the other republicans who had seen his true colors even before he took office. On the eve of his inauguration several republican leaders had visited him to remind him that he had once been a member of the Society of Jacobins. To their chagrin he answered, "Frankly, gentlemen, do you believe that a republic is possible in a country like ours? I thought 1793 had given France a lesson from which she profited.") As the years went on, Louis-Philippe had been emboldened to strengthen his so-called republican regime, and in the middle forties he had begun to tighten the laws prohibiting political meetings. In 1847 he sought to stifle criticism of his electoral laws, which, as Alexandre Ledru-Rollin's opposition newspaper, *La Reforme*, in-

Auguste Bonheur: *Rosa at Twenty-four*. Oil, 1846. Musée des Beaux-Arts, Bordeaux. ✿ This portrait was shown in the Salon of 1848 along with work produced by the Bonheur family. Raymond, his sons Isidore and Auguste, and his daughter Rosa submitted six drawings and two sculptures. "Our entries almost filled an entire page of the catalog," Raymond remarked proudly. Juliette was eighteen at the time and did not show until the Salon of 1852.

sisted, sponsored "the rule of France by purchased majorities."
His increasingly dictatorial gestures were felt even in the halls
of academe, where progressive professors such as Jules Michelet
and Edgar Quinet were suspended. When he began to seize
newspapers that criticized him, the educated classes took alarm.
A petition of two hundred thousand signatures for liberal reforms was presented, and, after a series of inflammatory ban-
quets, a large demonstration on February 22, 1848, initiated the
revolution. The following day, Louis-Philippe's troops fired on
the crowd, whose cry "Vive La Reforme!" quickly changed to
"Vive la République!" On the third day, the socialist Louis
Blanc appeared on the balcony of the Hôtel de Ville to announce
the formation of a republic, after having been serenaded by ten
thousand voices.

The first acts of the Second Republic on February 24 were to
abolish capital punishment, release all political prisoners, and, to
the delight of the art world, abolish the undemocratic jury system at the Salon. Ledru-Rollin, the new Minister of the Interior,
proclaimed that for 1848 all works sent to the Salon would be
accepted. Five days later he announced, "All artists are invited
to the School of Beaux-Arts on March 5 at noon to name a commission of forty members (fifteen painters, eleven sculptors, five
engravers, and four lithographers), who will be charged, together with the administration of the National Museum, with
the placement of works to be exhibited."

Eight hundred and one artists voted. The final commission
elected included a surprisingly broad spectrum of talents and
positions. The most votes (573) went to a conventional painter,
Léon Cogniet, who has sometimes been mistakenly called RB's
teacher. Ingres came in next with 551 votes; Delacroix won 546;
Horace Vernet 544; Alexandre Deschamps 541; Robert Fleury
539; Ary Scheffer 510; Ernest Meissonier 416; Camille Corot
353; and Paul Delaroche 324. Some 5,180 works were submitted
and had to be installed for the opening on March 15. The entire
Bonheur family took advantage of the occasion, filling almost an
entire page of the catalog, Auguste sent a portrait of Rosa, a still
life, and a portrait of a child. Isidore sent a canvas and a plaster
of a horseman attacked by a lion. Raymond submitted a landscape, and RB sent six paintings, including one of her most

widely noted works, *Cows and Bulls of the Cantal.* According to newspaper accounts, her cows were immensely successful with the crowds, who stood before her paintings every day. More important for her career, however, was the gold medal awarded her by the jury—which, as she said, reflected all the disparate tendencies of the time. Horace Vernet was president of the jury, and the other members were Cogniet, Delacroix, Meissonier, and Corot. Raymond wrote to Lacour describing the prize-award ceremonies, during which there were unanimous bursts of applause for his daughter. Horace Vernet even came over to shake her hand, giving her effusive compliments. While RB enjoyed a real triumph in terms of official success, especially because those who honored her were so distinguished, there was not unanimity among critics. She was to receive her first adverse criticism this time, and it would become increasingly acrid as the years went on. Clement de Ris, writing in the most popular artistic journal, *L'Artiste,* complimented her on the *Cows and Bulls of Cantal* in which she had avoided the dryness and meanness of touch of Brascassat. But he warned her to avoid using violent tonalities and avoid painting her fields in such detail. "To try to render each blade of grass is to practice the skill of the auctioneer, which has nothing to do with art."

The government of the new Second Republic began with high hopes for reforms in the system of art patronage. Early in March a general assembly of artists was held. Barye, the animal sculptor, who had always had trouble with official juries; Diaz, a landscape painter who had also fared poorly; and Couture asked that officials who had direct effect on the arts be elected by the whole body of artists. Delacroix and Deschamps were elected presidents of the artists' organization and set out their ideas for extensive reform. By May, however, the new government had recognized the futility of trying to answer the demands of the artists, and Charles Blanc, the new director of the Ecole des Beaux-Arts, refused to cede the power of his bureau. The government was besieged with requests for help, since, in the wake of the revolution in February, the art market had collapsed. In the mounting confusion, Charles Blanc attempted to honor the prevailing preferences in the artistic milieu. The 1848 commis-

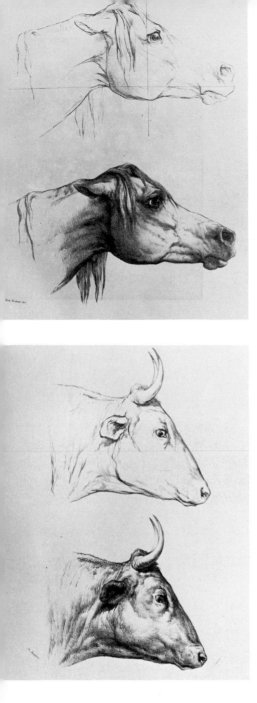

Rosa Bonheur: Studies of horses and oxen. Lithographs of Bonheur drawings, ca. 1847. Collection Mr. and Mrs. Harold F. Mueller. ✤ Neatly fitting into her ideals for a rural utopian existence, draft animals became one of Bonheur's early obsessions.

sion had given thirty-six prizes to genre painters, forty-three to landscape and animal painters, and only fifteen to history painters. So the republican government undertook to encourage the landscape and animal painters. It was a propitious time for RB. Not only had she carried away a coveted gold medal, but shortly after, she received a three-thousand-franc commission from the state for a painting on the subject of ploughing, a substantial sum compared to the five hundred francs received by the landscapist Charles Daubigny.

With her Salon success, RB felt she had satisfied her father's ambitions for her. "He really triumphed through me," she told her last biographer, Anna Klumpke. "Wasn't he my only professor? And then, too, to the legitimate satisfaction he had through being my teacher was added the other: that the government that thus glorified his daughter was the same that he loved and whose advent he had dreamed of."

With her life going so well, RB happily accepted the invitation of her father's friend, the sculptor Justin Mathieu, to visit him in the Nièvre. She wanted to base her commission painting on nature, and so she spent her time doing sketches in the field. She worked intensely in order to present it to the Salon of 1849; *Ploughing in the Nivernais* was to become one of her best-known paintings.

Her selection of the subject and the way she went about rendering it suggest that RB was at the time open to the new currents of thought that swept in during the Second Republic. The emphasis on democratic diversity had brought with it a new respect for "originality"—not only in the manner of painting but in the selection of motifs as well. Originality meant that an artist was relatively free to create whatever seemed worthy to him, thus relieving him of the responsibility of being "learned." The realists, together with the landscapists of the Barbizon school, gained a firm foothold during the first optimistic months of the Second Republic, and their success gave sanction to all painters who had abandoned the demands of learned painting on historic and allegorical subjects.

All the arts felt the impact of the revolution, including literature. RB may well have undertaken her *Ploughing in the Nivernais* after a careful reading of George Sand. In 1846 Sand had

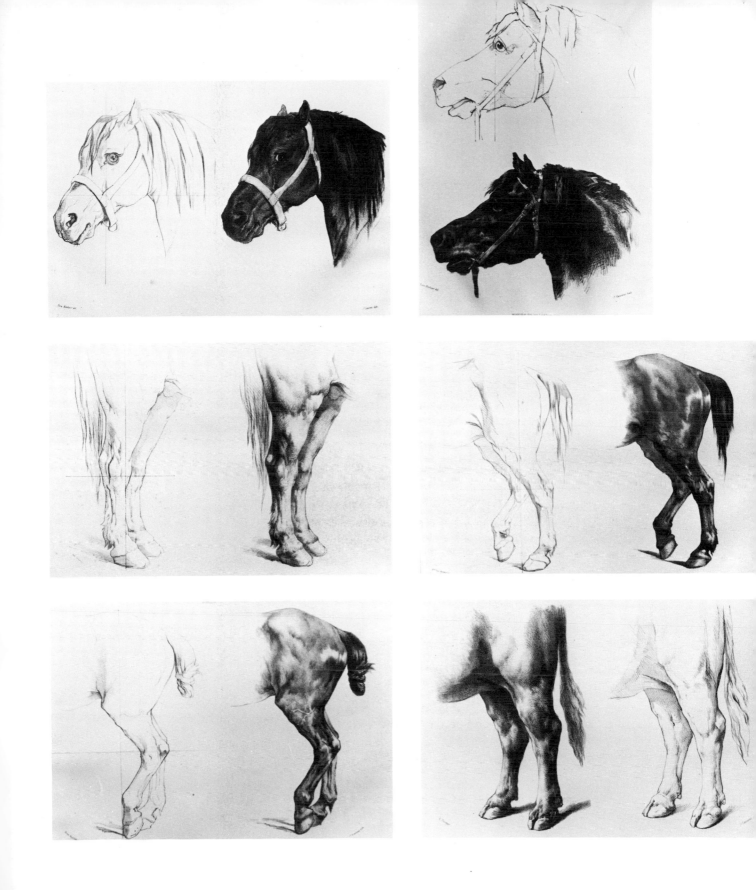

Rosa Bonheur: *Ploughing in the Nivernais*. Oil, 1849. Musée National du Château de Fontainebleau (173 × 260 cm). ❧ A signed copy of this painting, dated 1850, was sold to a M. Marc by RB a few years later for

4000 francs, half of which she gave to her brother Auguste for his collaboration in its reproduction. Ruefully, RB noted that she received 1000 francs more for the second version than she had for the original.

published one of the most celebrated of her pastoral novels, *La Mare au Diable (The Devil's Pool)*, in which she described the lives of the peasants and the cycles of nature in detail. The book had caused a stir and, as Sand herself noted, was regarded as "revolutionary." But, she wrote, no man ever effected a revolution. "I have not tried to invent a new language nor to affect a new style, though many newspaper articles have told me so." The popularity of the book became even more intense immediately after the revolution. Most artists and intellectuals entertained sentiments that were vaguely socialist and the glorification of labor became a fashionable motif. Several decades of rural Utopian socialist fantasies had prepared the public for the kind of sympathetic rendering of peasant life found in Sand's novels. She herself remarked that the novel had more to do with Virgil than with socialism, but commentators persisted in aligning her with the new revolutionary currents to the point that in 1851 she wrote a second preface insisting that she had merely meant to tell a simple story.

> The best an artist can hope for is to persuade those who have eyes to see for themselves. Look at what is simple, my kind reader, look at the sky, the fields, the trees and at what is good and true in the peasants; you will catch a glimpse of them in my book but you will see them much better in nature.

At the time that RB was casting about for her subject, according to Henry Bacon, she was listening to someone reading aloud from Sand's novel. At the passage that begins, "My attention was next caught by a fine spectacle, a truly noble subject for a painter," RB interrupted. "Yes," she exclaimed, "it would be a noble subject for a painting. George Sand is right. She must be fond of animals to describe them in so masterly a manner." The reader continued:

> At the other end of the field a fine-looking youth was driving a magnificent team of four pairs of young oxen, through whose somber coats glanced a ruddy, glowlike flame. They had short, curly heads that belong to the wild bull, the same large, fierce eyes and jerky movements; they worked in an abrupt, nervous way

that showed how they still rebelled against the yoke and goad and trembled with anger as they obeyed the authority so recently imposed. . . .

RB faithfully reflected Sand's ideal in her painting. Her father's basic teachings and Lammenais's sentimental attitude toward nature had prepared her for her task. She said in later years that when she undertook *Ploughing in the Nivernais*, she resolved "to paint a team of three pairs of oxen and, when I started to work, I had in mind also to celebrate with my brush the art of tracing the furrows from which comes the bread that nourishes all humanity." Her painting with its rich sienna foreground and heavy blue skies reflected her various influences, among them Paulus Potter and Géricault, while at the same time it announced her major focus, which was to be the expression of laboring animals. As always in her paintings, the human figures are awkward, as though they were an afterthought. Nevertheless, the painting stunned its Salon audience. The sentimental response is summed up by a commentator of the time, Eugène de Montrosier:

It chants the labor of the earth accomplished like a sacred rite by the peasant, sublime in his inferiority, the secret agent of the mysterious process of nature.

Ten years later, the critics were still discussing its power. Writing in *L'Artiste*, the critic Émile Cantrel praised RB's talents and compared her to George Sand. Both, he said, know how to listen to the mute symphonies of creation, and both know how to render them in the passionate and harmonious language of art. He concludes:

George Sand and Rosa Bonheur are two landscapists of the school of Jean-Jacques, two superior women that Europe envies us, two serious and committed painters whom France has the right to glorify—two brother geniuses.

In 1900, the *Gazette des Beaux Arts* was still discussing the painting that

> . . . produced a great sensation, both in the artistic world of Paris and among the general public, not only because of its affirmation of a masterliness of technique, of a virile strength of conception and execution, but also by virtue of the deep feeling that it expressed for the poetry of nature, and the intense love that it evidenced for the beings and the things pertaining to that nature.

The popular acclaim for Rosa Bonheur's painting brought her into favor with the broad coalition of artists and functionaries in official circles and guaranteed her a comfortable income. Certain artists, however, had their reservations. Eugène Delacroix, who had been on the 1848 jury and had praised her at the time, wrote in his journal the following year of a visit to Meissonier's studio when he had found Meissonier's faithfulness in representation "horrible."

> More and more I see, for my instruction and for my consolation, the confirmation of the thing Cogniet told me last year with reference to the *Man Devoured by a Lion* when he saw it alongside that of the cows by Mlle. Bonheur, which is to say that there is something else in painting beside exactitude and precise rendering from the model.

Many years later Paul Cézanne asked the dealer Ambroise Vollard what collectors thought of Rosa Bonheur. Vollard replied that it was generally agreed that *Ploughing in the Nivernais* was stunning. "Yes," replied Cézanne, "it is horribly like the real thing."

Nevertheless, in the 1850s, the officials and the bourgeois patrons continued to favor the real thing, and RB's career was successfully launched. She associated herself in 1849 with the Tedesco brothers, who were flourishing dealers. She also moved away from home and settled into a studio of her own, found for her by Mme. Micas on the rue de l'Ouest, where she hastened to meet the new demands created by her sudden success.

The death of Raymond Bonheur on March 23, 1849, distressed her greatly and rekindled the feelings of grief that her mother's death had so painfully inspired in her. Although she was twenty-seven years old, RB suffered the agonies of being an orphan. In her need for parental support, she turned to the staunch figure of Mme. Micas. Shortly after her father's death she asked to live with the Micas family, a gesture that permanently irritated her brothers and sister.

The following summer RB set off with Nathalie on a trip to the Pyrenees, the first of many such summer trips taken with the dual purpose of mending Nathalie's health and supplying RB with new material. Before leaving they applied for authorization to wear masculine clothing so that they could travel *en vrai cavaliers*. Both young women wrote long letters home describing their encounters with peasants, soldiers, and even bandits close to the Spanish border. RB filled many sketchbooks with studies of animals peculiar to the region and of the formidable mountains. When she returned, she set herself diligently to work composing paintings based on her sketches. Her new dealers could sell them without difficulty.

The affairs of the faltering Republic seem not to have disturbed her unduly. There is hardly a mention in her memoirs and recorded conversations, although the fall of the Republic in 1850 was to have considerable effect on her career. Charles Blanc had been forced to give up the ambitious program he had envisioned in 1848 as director of the Académie des Beaux-Arts. Then he had foreseen an end to pernicious "individualism" through the initiation of great public projects such as new industrial architecture, public sculpture and murals, works for railroad stations, and cooperatives to buy and distribute paintings. But, despite everyone's best intentions, the *juste-milieu* character and taste in the arts seemed to prevail. RB's tranquil landscapes and animals suited the ambivalent mood of the threatened Republic: she was neither too classical and fanciful, nor was she lacking in sentiment. Her subjects could be easily identified with the ideals of the new democracy, and her realism suited the prevailing interest in "scientific" attitudes toward nature. Her naïveté, as the critic Eugène de Mirecourt noted, appealed to a democratizing era in which the peculiarities of romantic individualism were rejected.

Although RB maintained that her father's influence had made her a permanently committed republican, she was able to make a quick transition when the Republic failed. She adjusted with ease to the new regime when Louis Napoleon was elected. She

Auguste Bonheur: *Raymond Bonheur at Fifty-three.* Oil, 1849. Klumpke. ❧ Painted the year of his father's death, this was one of Auguste's last portraits. From 1850 on, he followed in his sister's footsteps as an *animalier*, although he lacked her vigor and, as one critic complained, "He painted animals only on Sundays—after they had been groomed."

Rosa Bonheur's studio on the rue de l'Ouest. Lithograph, ca. 1849. From
Edmond Textier's *Tableau de Paris.* ❧ "And where have you ever seen
stables laid out in such a coquettish air?" wrote a M. du Pays in *L'Illustra-*
tion of Rosa Bonheur's first studio away from home. Describing the artist's
constant search for models "with four feet—with or without horns," he observed that "in Paris there are but few animals, only horses, dogs, and tom-
cats. . . . The beef, cows, and sheep only enter the city in the form of *filets,*
entrecôtes, et gigots."

72

was deeply flattered, it seems, when M. de Morny, the new Minister of the Interior, invited her to pay him a call.

It was shortly after the days of December. Several political friends of my father had been victims of the coup d'état, some exiled, others transported to Africa, where they died far from their families. I was very republican. All these events had profoundly upset me, and it was with a sort of inner trembling that I penetrated the office of the organizer of the coup d'état. I expected to find myself in the presence of a kind of tiger. To my stupefaction, I had to do with the contrary, a true gentleman, of imposing stature, filled with grace and distinction. His eye was lively, his mouth smiling. He expressed himself with elegance and perfect courtesy.

The Duc de Morny asked to see some of her sketches, and RB offered to bring a harvest scene and a horse-market scene. At the next audience he examined the sketches and told RB that since she was celebrated for her scenes of the life of cows and sheep, the state would order a country scene for the price of twenty thousand francs. So began RB's comfortable relationship with the builders of the Second Empire.

9.
Dawn of the Second Empire

Rosa Bonheur was not the only one to make an astonishingly swift adjustment to the new regime. The Second Republic's indecision had bred a spirit of disillusion that overtook even the most committed liberals who had so eagerly welcomed it. When Louis Napoleon was elected President for four years in December 1848, notables such as George Sand and Charles Augustin Sainte-Beuve were not unduly alarmed. His earlier history had persuaded them that he shared certain of the ideals of the 1848 revolution. Sainte-Beuve had even called him a "Saint-Simonian on horseback." Diligent years of myth-building by Louis Napoleon's sponsors had paid off.

Louis Napoleon's true character is still a matter of dispute. Some historians insist that he was at heart a socialist upholding Saint-Simonian ideals in trying to "improve the moral and material condition of the most numerous and poorest class." Others see his affection for socialist principles as purely philosophical,

Engraving from Edouard-Louis Dubufe's oil *Rosa Bonheur at Thirty-four*. 1857. Musée du Château de Versailles. ❧ While posing for this portrait, Rosa became vexed with its cloying flattery and lack of spirit. She asked Dubufe, a popular and sentimental portraitist "of the gentry," if, instead of the table he had placed by her arm, she could paint in her favorite bull herself. He dutifully accepted her offer and exhibited this finished version in the Salon of 1857. When an English collector of Paulus Potter works bought the painting, eight thousand francs went to Dubufe for the portrait and seven thousand francs to Rosa for the bull. "It was by way of gallantry to the lady," observed Dubufe, "because the bull was worth vastly more."

pointing to his numerous autocratic moves and his overweening imperial ambitions. His biography does not help to form a consistent image. Born in 1808 to Louis Bonaparte, King of Holland, and Hortense, Josephine's daughter by her first marriage, Louis Napoleon had a turbulent childhood in exile with his mother. In his youth he and his brother went to Italy, where they joined in a rebellion—a fact always stressed by his propagandists, who tried to show that his sympathies were courageously liberal even in his youth. After he was fetched from Italy by his alarmed mother, he settled down in Switzerland to write a treatise, *Political Reveries*, published in 1832. In it he offered a confused pastiche of Bonapartist notions that might have been read as liberal, since he supported a parliamentary constitution and the right of the people to approve by direct vote succession to the throne. On the basis of this treatise, Louis Napoleon established a small place for himself among Louis-Philippe's opponents. He followed his literary success with an abortive attempt to lead an uprising, for which Louis-Philippe deported him to New York. The following year he turned up in Victoria's England, where his reputation as a martyr gained him a few adherents, and by 1839, when he published his book *Some Napoleonic Ideas*, he had already framed his image as a man of destiny. His characterization of Napoleon in that book was as a "Messiah of new ideas" who was at heart a democrat. Had Napoleon not been harassed by wars and upheavals, Louis Napoleon claimed, he would have created a European state system with a single league of free men, a "holy alliance of peoples."

Emboldened by the modest success of his publications, Louis Napoleon tried another coup. This time Louis-Philippe was forced to imprison him. From his comfortable confinement at Ham, Louis Napoleon issued hundreds of cajoling letters to potential supporters. In 1844 he published a book, *Extinction of Pauperism*, that gained him the sympathy of some of France's most illustrious intellectuals. In it he argued that unemployment could be erased by transferring surplus labor to agricultural colonies formed to develop the waste lands of France. This version of a public-works project won approval with the less sophisticated political thinkers among the intellectuals. Both Béranger and George Sand were taken with the idea and wrote him congratulatory letters. It is not surprising, then, that a few years later, in June 1848, it was more the author of *Extinction of Pauperism* who was elected to the Assembly than the sly pretender to Napoleon's throne. In that confused election, Prince Louis Napoleon polled a substantial number of votes, but not as many as such avowed republicans and socialists as Pierre Leroux, Victor Hugo, and Pierre-Joseph Proudhon. Proudhon, writing a few days later, remarked:

> The people have just indulged in a princely whim: pray God it be the last! A week ago Citizen Bonaparte was still only a black dot in a fiery sky; the day before yesterday he was only a smoke-filled balloon; today he is a cloud bearing storms and lightning in its midst.

Proudhon's foreboding proved correct. The prince was elected President a few months later and lost no time putting his Napoleonic ambitions to work. His deputies fanned out through France warning the peasants and small provincial landowners against the "red specter" and began preparing the way for his final coup. Propaganda posters now bore the old Napoleonic emblems, and Louis's unprepossessing figure was redrawn to resemble his illustrious uncle. In December 1851 he was powerful enough to launch his coup d'état, to dissolve the assembly, and to call for a plebiscite, in which he was confirmed. Exactly a year later he crowned himself Emperor.

Despite his immediate moves to dissolve trade unions and control the press, the liberals still saw Louis Napoleon as a man of good will trying to reorganize France and reestablish the prosperity once known under Louis-Philippe. Even when he ordered that all the *Liberté, Egalité, Fraternité* signs be removed from public buildings, the liberals looked the other way. They told themselves that in spite of everything, his policies were generally liberal, and nowhere so obviously as in the arts. Many found it difficult to judge his real merits, among them Queen Victoria, who wrote in her diary:

> How far he is actuated by a strong *moral* sense of *right* and *wrong* is hard to say. My impression is that in all the apparently

inexcusable acts, he has invariably been guided by the belief that he is fulfilling a *destiny*.

Eventually even such liberals as remained hopeful had to concede that Louis Napoleon was a disaster. Many blamed the Empress, Spanish-born Eugénie de Montijo, for his increasingly reactionary acts. She was a royalist and a devout Catholic whose lifelong heroine was Marie Antoinette, and she never failed to urge her husband to rid himself of the more liberal advisers in his inner circle. The Empress did not entirely succeed, for Louis Napoleon needed the erstwhile liberals, especially the old Saint-Simonian engineers and financiers who had first begun to

Franz-Xavier Winterhalter: *The Empress Eugénie.* Oil, 1854. Metropolitan Museum of Art, New York; gift of Mr. and Mrs. Claus von Bülow, 1978. ✤ In this portrait, one of at least nine of the Empress painted by the famous German portrayer of royalty, Eugénie is dressed in a Louis XVI gown, one that she often wore to the masked balls given at the Tuileries.

build railroads in the mid-1840s. Now, with new financing and the support of the state, they could resume their ambitious schemes, which fostered greater employment. Middle-class investors found themselves boosted into the nobility, and many lesser figures could swagger in the streets of Paris safe in the knowledge that in Louis Napoleon's Empire, an enterprising businessman could well aspire to the aristocracy.

Louis Napoleon's regime proved no better or worse for artists than Louis-Philippe's. The middle-of-the-road artist flourished under the new government, whose chief, if indifferent, at least paid lip service to the importance of the arts. In Louis Napoleon's team were self-styled connoisseurs such as the Duc de Morny and Princesse Mathilde, who compensated for her brother's relative indifference by reinstituting the artistic private-salon tradition and collecting objets d'art and paintings. The imperial way of life did encourage an interest in the decorative arts, though the amplification of the bourgeoisie became a boon for the old socialist theorists who had advocated mass production as a means of equalizing society. Factories became devoted to making reproductions of precious objects in the Empress's palace, while rhetoricians spoke of egalitarian arts and crafts. Nevertheless, it is not difficult to understand the quick capitulation to the Second Empire of Rosa Bonheur and other artists, since it was quite clear that the new society was willing to acquire works of art and artisanship. As to the quality of those works, Charles Morazé summed it up in his 1966 study of the decorative arts:

> In all their reproductions, craftsmen were not content merely to excel; they wished to improve. Compare the imperial eagles of the First and Second Empires: the first made no claim to zoological accuracy, and was rather heraldic in inspiration; the second was a carefully observed copy of the eagle in the Jardin des Plantes. Scientific pretentiousness was substituted for an aesthetic sense.

Not surprisingly, the naturalistic tendency in painting found great favor with the new collectors who spurned the great ambitions of history painters and were content to buy picturesque genre paintings or scenes of landscapes and animals. In 1852 the Goncourt brothers, writing of sculpture, noted:

The historical school is dying in the art which makes things palpable just as is happening in the art which makes things visible. Landscape replaces it in painting, animals replace it in sculpture. Nature succeeds man. That is the evolution of modern art.

The critic Jules Castagnary, commenting on the Salon of 1857, noticed in its three thousand works that "It is the human side of art that substitutes itself for the heroic and divine side, and which affirms itself both with the power of number and the authority of talent." He attributed the disappearance of religious and history painting to social change and heartily approved of the new interest in genre painting.

Such social change favored the art of Rosa Bonheur, art that could be understood easily by the new middle-class patrons. She had come at the right moment. For more than a decade there had been constant shifts in attitude, and even the most opportunistic painters had had a hard time sorting out the various aesthetics. Gustave Flaubert portrayed the painter Pellerin in *L'Education Sentimentale* as panting to keep up with the times. First, in the early 1840s, Pellerin echoes the majority when he shudders at the new naturalism: "I don't want any of your hideous reality! . . . The cult of external truth reveals the vulgarity of our times; and if things go on in this way, art is going to become a bad joke inferior to religion in poetry and inferior to politics in interest. . . ." Later, Flaubert shows Pellerin belatedly acknowledging the basic principles of the romantic generation: "He had made considerable progress, for he had realized once and for all the stupidity of Line. One should not look for Beauty and Unity in a work of art so much as character and variety. 'Because everything exists in nature, and so everything is a legitimate subject for painting. . . .'" Finally, at the height of the Second Empire, Pellerin gained the fame he had sought by becoming a well-publicized photographer.

Much of the flourishing art trade was the result of the increasingly active role of entrepreneurs. RB was safely in the hands of the most enterprising art dealers, who had connections in England and particularly in America. Her lack of interest in the Salon in later years was due largely to the fact that she no longer needed such exposure in order to find clients. In fact, as Zola remarked in *L'Oeuvre*, the dealer "discourages his pet artist from showing in the Salon because the *new* clients seem to prefer the illusion of discovering the works for themselves, in a painter's luxurious and exotic studio." Thomas Couture, one of the painters who greatly benefited from the "new" clients, also mentions that the Americans particularly liked to visit studios so that they could feel they had found unknown artists. Despite her retiring nature, RB did collaborate with the dealers, particularly Ernest Gambart, in encouraging the new bourgeois patrons. She often received them in her Paris studio, which soon became a port of call for the Americans. She boasted later that in the early days of the Second Empire, Morny himself visited her studio several times, as did many of the newly titled members of the court.

In the beginning, the Second Empire with its stress on pomp and spectacle made for a certain gaiety, and everyone who was granted entrée to its inner circles seemed pleased enough with the enigmatic Emperor and his ambitious wife. It was during this time that RB, still young enough to be excited by her success, participated in the social life of Paris, meeting the highborn as well as her successful artistic colleagues. She was becoming known as an original character—a woman who rode her horse astride through the streets of Paris and who remained with the men after dinner to smoke her cigarette. Her ambitions and confidence were swelled by the attentions she received, and she resolved to paint a monumental masterpiece.

10.
The Horse Fair

In 1851, RB began to visit the horse market at Boulevard de l'Hôpital near the Asylum of la Salpêtrière. Since 1844, when a M. Richard had sent her a copy of his book, *Etude de Cheval*, she had been interested in perfecting her drawings of horses. She had learned their anatomy from this book and remembered the text many years later, quoting him: "Science is the key to nature's treasures. It reveals the infinite riches and marvels of the universe, which are an enigma for the ignorant."

Watching the handlers jogging horses at the market, she though of the frieze on the Parthenon. "My idea was not to imitate, but to interpret. In this spirit I made innumerable compositions and studies. I proposed to undertake this work on a canvas not less than 2.50 by 5 meters." RB's ambition and stamina were at their height in 1852. *The Horse Fair* demonstrated her ability to record the movements of animals in a way she had never managed before. In all likelihood her success derived from her decision to study very closely the works of her illustrious precedessor Théodore Géricault. Although she rarely mentioned Géricault to her biographers, she often followed his example. He had been the first French painter to frequent slaughterhouses and horse markets. He had gone to England, as RB was to do after *The Horse Fair*, and had shown great admiration for the same painters RB later sought out, foremost among them Sir Edwin Landseer. He had made countless drawings of horses in France, Italy, and England, often portraying them with scientific attention to detail. Above all, he had essayed his own

Parthenon frieze in his sketches and paintings for a composition he planned of the annual riderless horse race through the Roman corso.

During RB's student years the legend of Géricault was very much alive. Although few of his paintings were visible in public collections, there were hundreds of copies around and many lithographic reproductions. For French artists of 1850 "he was both little-known and very famous," as the art historian Lorenz Eitner says. "Today he would be bombastically labeled as 'underground.' " When the contents of Géricault's studio were sold, drawings and small oil studies were acquired by many artists, among them Delacroix and the animal sculptor Pierre Jules Mène, whom RB had met at the distribution of Salon prizes and whom she saw frequently.

There are many reasons to believe that RB was consciously planning a work in the grand manner of Géricault when she conceived of *The Horse Fair*. Her biographer Henry Bacon reported:

> Auguste Desmoulins told me that when he was leaving Paris for Algeria after the coup d'état in 1851 he went to bid adieu to Rosa and found her in her studio among many sketches in a larger, broader manner than her painting of years before. He expressed his delight, and without answering she moved her easel and showed a study of horses painted by Géricault which had been the sensation of Paris years before. The study had been lent to her and she was copying it for the purpose of better understanding the large manner of this master.

In fact, *The Horse Fair* was unique in RB's oeuvre. The "large manner" was abandoned shortly after, forever. It was not only in the painting technique that RB put herself to school with Géricault. In many of her studies of Percheron horses, she seems to have been inspired by certain very widely known Géricault prints. He had been making prints since 1817, the first known example of which is an etching of a Percheron. In 1821, during his visit to England, he worked for English publishers, producing among others the set "Various Subjects Drawn from Life and on Stone." Among the lithographs in this set are several depicting the heavy, rounded majesty of work horses. More important, there is a plate titled "Horses Going to a Fair" in which

(ABOVE) Rosa Bonheur: *The Horse Fair*. Oil, 1853. Metropolitan Museum of Art, New York; gift of Cornelius Vanderbilt, 1887 (244.5 × 406.8 cm).

(OPPOSITE) Rosa Bonheur: Sketches for *The Horse Fair*. Pencil, 1851–1852. Atelier, By. ❦ Flourishing after her recent successes at the Salons, Rosa centered her energies on what was to be her most ambitious and famous work—*The Horse Fair*. Twice a week she went to the horse market— always in male attire—in order to sketch the Percherons and their handlers in action. "This costume was a great protection to me," Rosa recalled years later. "My skirts would have been a great hindrance, making me conspicuous and perhaps calling forth unpleasant remarks. . . . Thus I was taken for a young lad, and unmolested."

Théodore Géricault: *Horses Going to a Fair*. Lithograph, 1821. Metropolitan Museum of Art, New York; Rogers Fund. ✢ Although Bonheur never spoke of Géricault's possible influence upon her, some critics did. *Study of a White Horse* by Géricault was one of the paintings in Rosa's art collection that sold at auction in Paris a year after her death.

a procession of Percherons is being herded by their grooms up a slope, filling the page with their generously rounded flanks. Interestingly, it was the young painter Léon Cogniet, whom RB knew in later years, who was commissioned to make a copy of this lithograph a year later for a French publisher. The print was published in reverse and, despite Géricault's dissatisfaction with its final state, was widely circulated.

Among Géricault's studies available in private collections in Paris RB may well have seen one or two dating from his stay in Rome, where he had been enthralled with the race on the corso. These studies varied from extremely faithful observations of the way the Roman grooms struggled to quiet their charges before the race to idealized versions of man and beast in classical Greek relationships. Many of the postures of the grooms were to be paraphrased in RB's *Horse Fair,* and the rhythmic disposition of the massed horses echoes Géricault's manner of composing. Since RB was far more comfortable generally with the new standards, in which composition was no longer considered a major concern in painting so long as the artist was scientifically correct in what he depicted, it seems likely that this unique, carefully constructed painting was inspired directly by Géricault.

There is much in Géricault's approach that would have made sense to RB. For one thing, he often made closely studied sketches of horses in which all "manner" was eschewed in favor of absolute accuracy. When he went to England he adopted the English penchant for genre scenes and was keenly interested in horse portraiture. Lorenz Eitner observes:

> It is curious to discover, in these horse portraits, that Géricault, so much given to tempestuous, expressive gestures when painting academic models or copying the masters at the Louvre, could assume an attitude of self-effacing objectivity when communing with nature in the stables.

RB's objectivity in *The Horse Fair* appears mainly in the exactitude of her rendering of the dusty cobbles and pebbles in the foreground and in the handling of the trees in the background. The rest of the painting is strongly affected by her interest in the romantic paintings of Delacroix and, above all, Géricault.

"Engraving of 'Horse Fair'— Free or for 15¢" ❧ ". . . A superb copy, printed upon the finest plate paper, nearly two by three feet" is offered of *The Horse Fair*—free of charge to every new subscriber in 1859— by the *United States Journal,* a publication devoted to "Agriculture, Mechanics, Literature and Current Events." "Every copy will be a magnificent specimen of art, forming a parlor ornament unsurpassed in interest by anything ever before issued on this side of the Atlantic."

Their influence can be felt in the way RB uncharacteristically uses rich color, linking the ends of her very long painting by means of cadenced accents, particularly in the strong blues of the clothing of four of the grooms. The romantic effects in her painting can be seen even more directly in the way she has strung together a series of small scarlet accents. At the extreme right she runs a bright red ribbon over a chestnut horse's flanks, then picks up the accent in the exact center of the painting on the rearing white horse's bridle, and suggests it again in the ribbon on the horse in the extreme left background.

The Salon of 1853 in which RB exhibited her *Horse Fair* was a resounding success in every way for her. Her painting was admired both by the critics and by the general public, who flocked to marvel at the painting's huge dimensions and the compelling interpretation of a scene familiar to them. Delacroix himself expressed his appreciation in his journal, noting that the jury could not award her a prize since she had already earned a first. He wrote, "Mlle. Rosa Bonheur has made an effort this year that is superior to those of previous years; one is reduced to encouraging her by voice and gesture."

Perhaps more important for her career was the response of the Emperor and Empress. They had been given a preview the day before the Salon opened, and, awed by RB's immense canvas, they expressed their pleasure to the officials in their entourage. The Emperor then went on to deliver himself of another artistic judgment on seeing Courbet's audacious *Nude Bather*, when he became incensed and rapped the canvas with his crop. (Courbet is said to have retorted, "If I had only foreseen this spanking, I should have used a thin canvas; he would have torn a hole in it

The Water Trough at the Horse Market in Paris. Lithograph, ca. 1847 (artist unknown). ✤ This lively scene of the horse market on Boulevard de l'Hôpital was sketched a few years before RB singled it out as the site for her painting *The Horse Fair.* The row of feathery trees and the cupola of the chapel of the old hospital of La Salpêtrière were to appear in the background of Bonheur's wide-angle composition.

and we should have had a splendid political lawsuit.") The Empress, seeing the monumental volumes of Courbet's bather, commented, "Is that a Percheron too?"

The imperial approval, coupled with the unusual popular response, made RB's reputation soar. A lithographic reproduction of the painting had phenomenal sales and spread her name throughout France, England, and eventually, in 1859, the United States. RB was well pleased with her fame, although she always maintained that it was too time-consuming. After the Salon, elated with her success, she decided to take Nathalie on one of their roving tours, this time to wild regions of the Pyrenees which they had not yet visited. Writing to her sister from Cautets near the Spanish border, she said:

> Fame is not without its inconveniences, as well as its agreeable side. Up to now I have succeeded in keeping my incognito, but at present I am receiving cards from all quarters and my hotel landlord is so proud to have me in his house that he walks about the streets singing my praises.

Her high spirits at the time can be gauged by the anecdotes contained in the same letter:

> All the country people like me and the Spanish men look at me with a favorable eye. Mariano, the famous smuggler, whom it is impossible to capture, he is so clever and so much dreaded, and who says he has never sat for his portrait to anyone but me—what an honor!—has been to lunch with me at the hotel. In spite of the mistrust he inspires in me, he appears to have taken a fancy to me and goes about the country saying he would give his life for me.

She goes on to say she has even tamed "a wilder specimen," a man who never remained in the town for more than an hour at a time, the famous smuggler Navarros. He, too, sat for her and allowed her "to become acquainted with his tiger's smile—a thing rare enough. . . ."

Early in September she reported to her brother Isidore that she had been making a rough sketch of some smugglers and had managed to acquire a few Havana cigars—smuggled ones—for him.

11.
Fame and Fortune

When RB came back to Paris in the fall of 1853 she returned as a famous artist, full of confidence and economically secure. Her *Horse Fair* was still drawing great attention. Few paintings have had such a strong public impact. Its fortunes and her own, as she always said loyally, were directed by the art dealer Ernest Gambart, whose phenomenal success in the Victorian era warranted the title his biographer, Jeremy Maas, bestowed upon him, "Prince of the Victorian Art World." Gambart had begun his career working for the Paris firm of Goupil, for whom he went to England in 1840. The situation of the art market there kindled his entrepreneurial gifts. The English aristocrats, formerly the main source of support for artists, were no longer buying very much, but there were new patrons to be developed among the tycoons of the newly industrialized Midlands. Gambart's fortune would be made, as Maas points out, by the "cutlers and cotton kings in the forties, the druggists and textile merchants in the fifties, and the ironmasters of the sixties and seventies."

From 1851, the time of the Great Exhibition in London, until 1873, financial speculation and industrial growth developed a prosperous middle class eager to acquire culture. Artists were able to survive and in some cases to flourish thanks to the system such dealers as Gambart devised whereby artists would sell both the original painting and the copyright that guaranteed widespread sales of reproductions. This system worked very much in RB's favor. Maas notes that "the very foundations of the print trade rested on the simple distinction crucial to an understanding of the Victorian art world in general. . . . On the one hand there was the picture, and on the other the copyright. Each might be sold as a separate entity."

Gambart realized that he could enlarge the English market for modern French artists by introducing not only prints but also original works. His first London exhibition was of the animal bronzes of RB's friend and mentor, Pierre Jules Mène. Then, in 1851, he staged a large foreign exhibition in which he included RB's painting *Charcoal Burners in Auvergne Crossing a Moor*, which drew favorable comment. The poet-painter Dante Gabriel Rossetti called it "*the* best work in the place." After the sensation of the Salon of 1853 and *The Horse Fair*, Gambart decided to establish a close working relationship with RB, commencing a lifelong friendship that would prove mutually beneficial. In his memoirs, Gambart wrote:

After the closing of the Salon, *The Horse Fair* was sent to the Society of Artists of Gand for exhibition in that city and did not find a buyer. I informed myself during the Spring of 1854 during a visit to Mlle. Bonheur of what had become of her large painting and offered to buy it. It was then on exhibition in Bordeaux, her

Pierre-Jean David d'Angers: Rosa Bonheur medallion. 1854. Atelier, By. ⚜ A year after her successful showing of *The Horse Fair*, Rosa joined the gallery of the celebrated—Victor Hugo, Alfred de Vigny, Delacroix, Balzac, Lamartine, Harriet Beecher Stowe, and hundreds of others—executed in bronze by the leading medalist of the age.

Pierre Jules Mène: *Group of Animal Bronzes*. Atelier, By. ⚜ The trading of quadripeds was busy business among the *animaliers* of the nineteenth century and was often the *raison d'être* for the exchange of letters between them. The prolific correspondence between Bonheur and Mène chronicles many of the animals' comings and goings. Having returned a feisty billy goat to the sculptor, RB wrote to Mène's wife in 1860 of a new tenant in her menagerie: "I have here another object which might interest that other star whose hairy rays are silvered [Mène]. I can show him an elk which has just been sent me from America and which, though a female, is not without merit."

Rosa Bonheur: Studies for *The Horse Fair*. (CLOCKWISE FROM UPPER
LEFT) Oil, undated. Art Institute of Chicago; gift of USY and T. Industries (43.2 × 87 cm). ❧ Watercolor, 1867. Knoedler, New York
(63.5 × 128.2 cm). ❧ Black chalk, gray wash on beige paper, undated. Metropolitan Museum of Art; bequest of Edith H. Proskauer,
1975 (13.7 × 33.7 cm). ❧ Pencil, undated. Collection Mr. and Mrs.
Harold F. Mueller (27 × 41 cm).

native city. She wanted very much that the municipality acquire it for the museum. She had offered it for the price of 12,000 francs [$2,400 at the time]. She told me that if the painting returned, she would gladly let me have it but not at 12,000 francs, as it would have to leave France.

In a letter in later years to the American collector Samuel P. Avery, who eventually bought the painting, Gambart was more specific, saying that the city of Bordeaux did refuse. Gambart then offered to have the painting engraved by Thomas Landseer and came up with the full sum of 40,000 francs that RB demanded if the painting left France. He planned to star the painting in his 1855 exhibition, but in the meantime Landseer was to undertake the engraving. RB, pleased with the idea of the reproduction, had second thoughts about her hard bargain: "I don't wish to abuse your liberality. How can things be arranged? The canvas is very large and I think it will be difficult to fit it in an engraver's atelier. Wouldn't it be better if I made you a smaller copy?" Gambart naturally assented, and she added, "I will give you a reproduction and that will calm my conscience. I can say that I sold my painting for 40,000 francs and I will not have victimized you too much."

They agreed that she would make a copy one-quarter the size of the original and send him the original as well for the agreed-upon price. Gambart lost no time putting the reduced copy in the hands of Thomas Landseer. Jacob Bell, a collector of Edwin Landseers, saw the picture and bought it for 25,000 francs. When Gambart's French exhibition opened in London on May 1, 1855, the large version had not yet arrived, but Gambart had insured the success of his exhibition by preparing the ground with the royal family; he had staged an earlier charity show in which a work by the fifteen-year-old Princess Royal, Victoria, had sold for 400 guineas. This judicious move insured the presence of Queen Victoria and Prince Albert at the inauguration of his French exhibition. However, even their august presence did not stir the British public until the day in June when Gambart finally was able to install the original *Horse Fair*. The response in the press was "a unanimous concert of admiration." The Queen had it brought to Windsor Castle for a private viewing.

This instantly bestirred the public, and Gambart's gallery was besieged with visitors.

Toward the end of the show, William P. Wright, an American, offered to buy the painting for 30,000 francs, leaving Gambart free to have it exhibited in America for three years. Wright paid 10,000 on account, the rest to be paid after the three years were up. When Gambart's agent later went to collect the balance, however, Wright claimed a share of the profits from the traveling exhibition and after much discussion paid only 13,000 francs. Gambart lamented the fact that he received only 25,000 francs in the sale of the quarter-size reproduction and only 23,000 francs for the large work. However, he did admit that the publication of the engraved reproduction was more fruitful and that the traveling exhibition had provided a solid base for Bonheur's sales in America.

In 1859 the quarter-size reproduction was bequeathed by Jacob Bell to the National Gallery in London. RB was distressed because she had let Nathalie Micas do a great deal of the underpainting, and so she painted another copy, this time prepared by her sister, Julierre, and offered it to the National Gallery. It was regretfully refused because of the terms of Bell's will. In the catalog the Bell copy is listed as by both RB and Jeanne Sarah Nathalie Micas, "a painter of Hispano-Portuguese origin." The other copy was sold to a Mr. Mac-Connel. There was also a smaller watercolor copy in existence, so that, as Gambart noted, there were, in effect, five *Horse Fairs*. In his letter to Samuel Avery he says that he offered to repurchase the large *Horse Fair* for 50,000 francs in 1871 but was outbid by the American millionaire A. T. Stewart. The picture remained in the Stewart collection until March 25, 1887, when Avery purchased it on behalf of Cornelius Vanderbilt for the sum of $53,000. Vanderbilt presented it to the Metropolitan Museum, where it still resides.

In her notes for *The Horse Fair*, Margaretta Salinger mentions that the date 1853 is followed by the numeral 5, "which might indicate that the artist, responding to criticism made at the time of the exhibition, retouched certain passages and extended the date to 1855." Comparing the original with a contemporary engraving, Salinger suggests that the parts repainted were the ground, trees, and sky, which is likely since, in her sharp focus on animal representation, RB had never really come to terms with landscape. The broad manner adopted for the representation of the horses did not carry over in her depiction of the surroundings, and even in the final version the weakest painting is to be found in the ground and foliage.

In the United States, RB's reputation was greatly enhanced as her painting made its three-year tour. The American art journal *The Crayon* announced in October 1857 that the picture had finally arrived in New York. The following month the Boston column in *The Crayon* stated, "we quite envy New York the possession of Mlle. Rosa Bonheur's *Horse Fair*" and wondered if there was a possibility for it to come to Boston. Whether it did or not is unclear, but in 1858 it was shown in New Orleans and several other cities. In the meantime, Gambart did not let RB's name languish in London. In his 1858 French exhibition, her portrait of the dog Barbaro was admired greatly, one critic writing that Barbaro "is a dog in every sense of the word and is painted just as I would like to be painted if I were a dog."

RB's astonishingly rapid success after 1853 enabled her to indulge in her expensive passion for surrounding herself with a menagerie. "Today," wrote the critic Armand Baschet in 1854:

> Mlle. Rosa Bonheur has left rue de l'Ouest and chosen, with perfect taste, a garden and an adjacent building for herself. She has made of the garden a courtyard with palisaded stables. The vast window of her studio, with superb light, faces this courtyard where her heifer, her goats, and her sheep, as well as her mare, Margot, can live freely. If you add to this fantastic menagerie all the fowl of a Normandy farm, you will see that I exaggerate little when I say that for Paris, the domain of Mlle. Rosa Bonheur could be taken for a real model farm.

The new studio on the rue d'Assas, which the Micas family had supervised in construction, was grand and fully equipped. It was admirably suited to the period in RB's life when she was most active socially and when she was still flattered by the appearance of important socialites in her preserve. "My Fridays at the rue d'Assas were brilliant," she frequently recalled in later years. Numerous visitors came to marvel at her collection of animals and to get a glimpse of the artist herself, already much discussed for her unconventional dress and her habit of riding Margot astride through the streets of Paris. If the visitors wished to see her works they were often disappointed. After *The Horse Fair*, RB's dealers, Gambart and the Tedescos, were ever at hand with commissions and promised sales, and they quickly carried away whatever she finished. Baschet described seeing many studies of quadrupeds, sketches of mountain goats and troops of sheep, but very few finished works. The same was true in another studio that RB kept in the suburb of Chevilly. The walls were covered with sketches, but there were never any finished works. She obviously fell in with the ambitious programs of her dealers without difficulty. Never did she torment herself with the kinds of arguments that could be heard in the Parisian cafés attended by the new generation of painters. The problems of art-for-art's-sake, or of originality, were far from her concerns. Working to order did not offend her sensibilities, nor did the repetition of motifs that dealers demanded seem in any way inhibiting to her.

Life at the rue d'Assas was largely regulated by the Micas family. RB was sheltered from all household problems and spent her days at work in the splendid new studio. Often in the late afternoons she would ride to the Bois de Boulogne or pay calls on some of her eminent friends. Her new economic prosperity enabled her to indulge her need to collect animals, and sometimes this obsession resulted in tragicomic household conflicts. Her brother-in-law especially recalled an otter that she had brought back from the Pyrenees. "This otter was the despair of Mme. Micas for he had the bad habit of leaving the water—Rosa had installed a tank for him—and getting in between the sheets of Mme. Micas' bed."

This was the most gregarious period in RB's life, and many who knew her then have left revealing descriptions of her appearance and behavior. Her lifelong friend, the painter Paul Chardin, accepted an invitation to visit her at the studio and reported, "She was just dismounting from her horse and was attired in a sort of masculine costume that was really grotesque. It consisted of a frock-coat, loose gray trousers with understraps, boots with spurs, and a queer hat." The son of the sculptor

Rosa Bonheur: Sketches of animals. Klumpke. ✤ "I became an animal painter because I loved to move among animals," Rosa told a fellow artist. "I would study an animal and draw it in the position it took, and when it changed to another position I would draw that."

David d'Angers remembered seeing her often in his father's studio. His most vivid recollection, though, was of seeing her on horseback:

> She was in masculine dress. Her trousers had bootstraps, the last pair of the kind I remember seeing. Her cap was the queerest part of her odd getup. It reminds me of those sometimes worn by the lady bicyclists of the present day. She was naturally short, and the cut of the jacket made her look still shorter in the saddle. The ensemble of the costume was not happy.

On the other hand, a contemporary journalist offered a more flattering description, calling her "a young woman, small and delicate looking, with straight, strong lines in her features, a large square forehead framed in heavy hair cut short like a young man's, and with black, lively, flashing eyes." Others often remarked on her small feet, to which she herself would call attention, pointing out that she always wore expensive, soft, and very feminine boots.

Despite her ambitious production program, RB found time during the 1850s to carry on the work her father had begun when he had assumed the directorship of a drawing school for girls in 1848. Assisted by her sister, Juliette, RB taught what she called "the science of drawing," in which she advocated her father's principle of direct observation. To this she added her own system of analytic study. Her teaching program took cognizance of the new roles possible for women artists in industrialized society. She had always said that women were the equals of men even in the public arena of the arts, and part of her ambition for her students was to prove through them the efficacy of her father's old Saint-Simonian views.

When ceremonies were held at the end of one year, RB invited Arsène Houssaye, an erstwhile admirer of the Saint-Simonians and now Inspector General of the Beaux-Arts, to deliver the speech. His views clearly showed how the original Saint-Simonian doctrines could be adapted to the Second Empire's ambitions. Houssaye urged his listeners to take notice of the burgeoning manufacturing industries and to lend their designing talents to the factories. He exhorted them to "open their

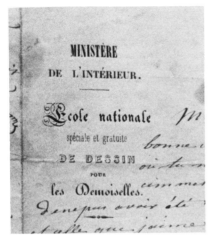

Letterhead of the Bonheur drawing school. Atelier, By. ✤ "Her pupils fear her, but at the same time they are very fond of her," the Paris correspondent for *The Crayon* wrote in 1858. "I have no patience with women who ask permission to think," Rosa warned her pupils. "Let women establish their claims by great and good works, and not by conventions."

imaginations to all the fantasies that accompany industry but are still art." This proto-Bauhaus vision of the role of artists was acceptable to RB, who wished to make her charges the equal of men in every endeavor. It may also explain her own acquiescence to the production-line demands of her dealers. Her attempt to infuse her charges with masculine pride is reflected in her often harsh criticisms of their work. Her way of scolding them was to tell them, "Go home to your mother and mend stockings or make petit point."

Her views were shared by others. During the year of the Exposition Universelle of 1855 the spectacle of thousands of paintings shown alongside industrial exhibits drew great crowds and much favorable comment. The Emperor had taken care that the exposition rival the 1851 British Great Exhibition by appointing a special commission to study the British techniques. The underlying motif of the Paris Exposition was meant to stress the natural alliance between art and industry, though paradoxically,

Isidore Bonheur: *Lion Attacking a Gavial Crocodile.* Terracotta, 1860. Hirshhorn Museum and Sculpture Garden, Smithsonian Institution, Washington, D.C. ✤ Making his debut in the Salon of 1848 with a sculpture called *Horseman Attacked by a Lioness,* Isidore Bonheur soon adopted animal duels as his principal theme. "Dodore," as she loved to call him, was RB's favorite brother. On June 24, 1861, RB wrote a friend: "As regards Isidore, he too has much talent, only, like his sister, he is more a builder of castles than a doer of deeds."

Rosa with her brothers and sister. Ca. 1852. ⚜ Seated: Auguste and Rosa; standing: Juliette and Isidore. "What I want is for us to be known as the three Bonheurs," Rosa wrote enthusiastically to her brother Isidore in 1850. "As for Juliette, she has too much of the motherly instinct in her for my taste, and I am afraid she will get more happiness out of having children than from an artistic career." Juliette had a small success at the Salons as an *animalier* and bore two sons, both of whom became artists.

Rosa Bonheur: *Haymaking in the Auvergne.* Oil, 1855. Musée National du Château de Fontainebleau (313 × 654 cm).

through the Emperor's ambitions, the old Saint-Simonian dream was to be realized.

In the vast spaces of the halls given over to the fine arts, another of the old Saint-Simonian notions—that of the primacy of labor—was fortified by the deliberate selection of landscapes, many of them scenes of farm labor. RB submitted *Haymaking in the Auvergne,* which won her a gold medal and wide attention in the press. Even the American art press was alerted when the London correspondent for *The Crayon* reported:

That wonderful woman Rosa Bonheur contributes to the French exposition here; a woman I imagine unprecedented in Art for vigor and ability armed at all points. A sketch by her of two calves is among the most admirable things I know of a truthfulness and thence a beauty, quite touching.

Marveling at her success, Anatole de LaForge wrote that the ensemble of her works could be called a "Hymn to Work." Her various paintings of sowing, harvesting, and ploughing, he said, treat the labor of animals and men with equal respect. Another critic, A. M. Mazure, wrote that after the old Dutch painters, the French had produced several painters of animals such as Brascassat and Troyon, but above all, a genius called Rosa Bonheur. In the mid-1850s, then, RB's work was seen in the context of the rural genre painting then very much in vogue, with its somewhat sentimentalized vision of peasant labor and its softened versions of domestic animals. Courbet's message, delivered with such aplomb during the Exposition when he erected his own "temple of realism," was not yet quite understood. RB, on the other hand, had gained wide public attention and approval, as can be judged by the frequent mention of her name in correspondences and journals of the period. Even the young Monet, for instance, anticipated being impressed by her work when as a seventeen-year-old he made his first trip to Paris. But he was disappointed. He wrote to his old mentor, Boudin, in February 1856, mentioning his excitement at seeing the works of Delacroix, Millet, and Rousseau, and commented, "I will tell you that after all of that, the Troyons don't hold and the Bonheurs still less."

12.
The Grand Tour
of Britain

In London, Ernest Gambart, after producing the sensational *Horse Fair* in 1855 and engaging the interest of the Queen, decided the next year to follow up his success by producing Rosa Bonheur herself. His talents as a showman were indisputable, although they sometimes won him the anger of frustrated artists. After a falling-out, Rossetti wrote a limerick for him:

> There is an old he-wolf named Gambart
> Beware of him if thou a lamb art
> Else thy tail and thy toes
> And thine innocent nose
> Will be ground by the grinders of Gambart

Nonetheless, Gambart knew how to promote his artists and how to cajole and retain the interest of the rich and powerful.

Gambart's proposal was received with joy by RB, who had long been encouraged by tales of the English sympathy for *animaliers*. She agreed immediately to come and was especially happy that Gambart had thoughtfully planned a trip to Scotland, home of her favorite authors, Walter Scott and the legendary Ossian. She arrived with Nathalie at Dover late in July 1856. Gambart immediately whisked them to a country house in Wexham, an old rectory rented by him for the occasion.

Events during this important trip were carefully orchestrated. Gambart persuaded Sir Charles Eastlake, who was then President of the Royal Academy, to offer a large dinner party in RB's

Frederick Goodall: *Rosa Bonheur at Work near Wexham.* Oil, 1856. Collection Morton Bradley. (Photograph: Heidi Katz.) ❧ "Mrs. Gambart gave me permission to paint her while she was painting the cattle," the English genre painter Goodall wrote in his diary while he was a member of the traveling Bonheur retinue. "While doing so she put out her little foot under her dress and begged me to take notice of it, as it was so small. It was the opinion of many people who had never met her that she was a masculine woman. I can say with truth that she was quite the reverse. Her hands and feet were *petites;* her face was not strictly beautiful, or fine, or handsome; but her expression was so vivacious and intelligent that I thought her charming."

Rosa Bonheur: *Sir Edwin Landseer* (1802–1873). Photograph, ca. 1856. ❧ Elegantly dressed in country tweeds, Edwin Landseer, dean of English animal painters and protégé of Queen Victoria, sat for his studio portrait in front of a ruggedly painted landscape. Although a confirmed bachelor, Landseer was so taken by Rosa's charisma that he gallantly offered to become "Sir Edwin Bonheur." The joke soon backfired as rumor of the impending marriage raced through the London art world.

honor. Lady Eastlake in her diary entry for Monday, July 16, noted that RB had been especially delighted to meet Edwin Landseer, whose work she so much admired. He, in turn, "was full of impudence, counted up to eight bachelors, and sent a deputation of marriage to her adding that he would be 'only too happy to become Sir Edwin Bonheur.'" The following day Lady Eastlake reported that Gambart hung the original *Horse Fair* in his gallery, where distinguished guests had been invited to meet "the female Landseer." On July 18, Lady Eastlake fulfilled RB's long-cherished dream and took her to visit Landseer's studio. In her journal Lady Eastlake wrote:

> Her whole enthusiasm as a woman [has] been long given to Landseer. Engravings of his works were the first things she bought with the money she earned; and in his house, surrounded by the most exquisite specimens of his labor and his skill—studies without end of deer, horses, Highlanders, tops of Scotch mountains, etc.: and with him pulling out one glorious thing after another, calling her first to one room and then into another . . . his dogs about him and a horse, tame as a dog, handed into the painting room—she was in a state of quiet ecstasy.

During the visit Landseer presented RB with two engravings. She was so moved that she blushed and burst into tears.

Each day of the momentous English visit was filled with lunches, dinners, endless toasts, and encounters with important people. Both Nathalie and RB were elated. RB responded to the adulation with a burst of pride and energy. She planned new works and began keeping extensive notebooks. In a letter to her sister, Juliette, from Wexham dated August 8, 1856, she expressed her satisfaction and her feeling of inspiration in unusually lyrical terms:

> I went yesterday and visited the park and forest of Windsor. People talk of trees at Fontainebleau. But here you have the same ancient forest monarchs.
>
> In Windsor Park I saw a very pretty subject for a picture. Under some gigantic oaks was a herd of 200 deer. So I stopped the carriage and Gambart and I began to approach them stealthily in order to see them close to. To my astonishment, instead of taking

flight they executed a most important piece of maneuvering. All the males formed themselves into a close battalion and formed a front of splendid antlers carried with the utmost gravity and pride. Meanwhile all the females and the young ones ran and took up their position behind this advance guard. Then, to amuse ourselves we deviated to the left, when the band of female deer ran immediately to the right while the males looked at us with a martial air. . . .

Gambart was a gallant companion. RB wrote home commenting on his assiduous attentions to his wife and to all the ladies. He carefully planned the trip to Scotland, so much longed for by RB. (Here she was inspired by Sir Edwin Landseer's example. In 1824 the painter C. R. Leslie had taken him to the Highlands and introduced him to Walter Scott at Abbotsford. His long series of stags and other wild life of the Highlands dated back to this visit.) En route to Scotland, Gambart had planned a kind of publicity campaign so that at Birmingham, for example, their train was met by a horde of children massed around the station presenting bouquets and an address of welcome.

Finally, at Liverpool, they embarked for Greenock. RB was very happy, she told Gambart, to reach the country of Ossian, to whom she owed so many inspirations. She was busy making sketches all along the Inverary road toward Loch Eck. The road took them to various lochs, including Loch Katerine of "Lady of the Lake" fame. At the end of August, they passed two weeks at Loch Leven, where again she busied herself noting the characteristics of Scottish oxen and sheep. Gambart knew she would be stimulated by a visit to the Falkirk Fair due to open September 9, and so she was, according to his account:

> The annual Falkirk Fair was close at hand and every day at low tide herds of oxen, coming thither from the north, crossed the firth swimming, escorted by two or three boats with shepherds in them and drovers, who guided the animals to the further bank and now and again upheld them by their horns if they were in danger of drowning. . . .

Gambart was right to imagine RB's tremendous excitement when she saw the animals struggling through the water and the

MLLE. ROSA BONHEUR.

The "French Landseer" Painter of the "Horse Fair" &c.

W. H. Mote: *Mlle. Rosa Bonheur.* Engraving, ca. 1857.
❧ During her triumphal travels through England and Scotland in 1856, Bonheur was given the sobriquet of "The French Landseer" by the well-disposed English press.

(RIGHT) Rosa Bonheur: *A Camp in the Moonlight.* Charcoal, 1868. Klumpke. ⚜ Inspired by her readings of the legendary bard Ossian, Bonheur made many drawings on this theme after visiting Scotland.

(BELOW) Rosa Bonheur: *The Crossing of Loch Leven.* Pencil and crayon, 1867. Musée National du Château de Fontainebleau.

agitated movements of their shepherds. She was also moved by the scenes of flocks of sheep being ferried from one island to another, and both swimming oxen and sheep found their way into her later paintings. Gambart continued his account in his memoirs:

> When we visited Falkirk Fair we drove from a friend's house in a wagonette. Our arrival created quite a sensation, for, beside our own party, there were two distinguished members of the Royal Academy.... This sensation was increased when Rosa Bonheur pointed out from her carriage six animals, a young bull and five splendid oxen, which she wanted to buy and take away with her. Instead of separating them quietly from the herd, the drovers began to strike right and left in order to get them out more quickly. This caused a panic during which the cattle crushed several sheep of the flock....

The Scottish lochs and mists very much suited RB, whose letters were filled with exclamations. She wrote to Juliette:

> For just a month we have been climbing mountains and crossing waters without resting.... I have seen all the places Walter Scott had chosen for the characters he created, especially those of the Legend of Montrose.... I am bringing back a cargo not of studies but of living animals....

The final stop on the Scottish tour was the Isle of Arran where, she wrote, "we climbed to the top of the highest peak, whence a view is obtained simultaneously of the north of Scotland, of Ireland, of England and of Wales. And such beautiful sea tints and skies." As usual, Gambart had managed to get up a splendid dinner party. One of the guests recorded her impressions:

> I remember the enthusiastic admiration of the celebrated Rosa for the grandeur of the island scenery and how... she expatiated loudly and with much gesticulation on its wonderful beauty. Then, suddenly addressing the Mater in English she, reaching her arms out dramatically to the range of the mountains beyond the sea, cried, "O magnificent! O beautiful! O grand! O very well!..."
> Rosa was of commanding presence and looked essentially a

(TOP) Rosa Bonheur: Sketch of oxen in Falkirk. Ink, 1856. Atelier, By. ❦ "Everyone knows that Rosa is going to the Falkirk Fair," Nathalie Micas wrote her mother from Scotland, complaining of the lack of privacy they were experiencing. "She is followed or escorted by 200 persons; if celebrity has its good side it is sometimes awfully annoying and tiresome."

(BOTTOM) Rosa Bonheur: *Two Scotch Herdsmen Leading a Bull.* Charcoal, undated. Collection Mrs. Michael P. Lawrence (51 × 40 cm). ❦ This sketch was probably made during RB's peregrinations through the Scottish Highlands. She wrote her sister in August 1856: "Now I know Scotland pretty well. You meet with nothing but MacGeorges, Macdonalds, and Macs of all sorts, *real* bare-legged mountaineers."

being above the common herd. Her dress was a compromise between that of a woman and a man; she wore her hair in a brown curly crop, and she rode horseback astride, to the horror of all kirk-going folk. . . .

The memory of the Scottish trip never dimmed for RB. In 1897 she wrote a letter in which she recalled England and Scotland, "a superb country in spite of its melancholy mists; for I prefer what is green to what is scorched. . . . I love the Scotch mists, the cloud-swept mountains, the dark heather—I love them with all my heart."

All through the journey RB kept bringing the party to a halt in order to record a vista or some animals in her notebooks. Gambart said she had encountered cows, bulls, and sheep such as she never saw in France and was eager to record their features. She was very lively in all respects and pleased her hosts with her general inquisitiveness. Once the party visited an ancient forge that excited her imagination. Nathalie wrote her mother about "the oldest foundry in the entire world" and mentioned that the fires had been burning for two hundred years, night and day. With her more pronounced interest in technology, she described the procedure and amounts of metals produced and added that it had been one of the most interesting days of their tour.

At the end of September, RB took Nathalie back to Paris and returned alone to England a few weeks later. Gambart, it seemed, had still more plans for promoting her fame. He had arranged for John Ruskin to dine with them. In Gambart's view, a dinner with Ruskin, who was already renowned as a critic, would have singular benefits for RB. On October 20, Ruskin noted laconically in his journal, "Pleasant evening with Rosa Bonheur," and on November 12, "again saw Rosa Bonheur (near Slough)." Apparently Ruskin himself had asked Gambart to arrange the meeting "to talk about art." He probably knew little of RB's work at the time, but, in the few works he had seen, he had noticed affinities with the English painters who interested him. A few years before, he had been drawn to the Pre-Raphaelites, who, in their opening manifesto, had committed themselves "to encourage and enforce an entire adherence to the simplicity of nature." Their concern with directness and accurate detail had impressed Ruskin, who himself made dry, closely detailed watercolors.

If Ruskin responded to the meetings with RB with only a few words in his journal, others kept far more complete notes. Gambart reported that Ruskin's arrival turned the little village of Wexham upside down:

Two days before, his servant came to hire rooms for him and as the furniture was not considered suitable, some better had to be gathered from Windsor. A cook came down also in order to prepare his breakfast and when Mr. Ruskin himself entered the village it was with his own carriage and domestics, the railway being disdained.

During the dinner, also attended by the painter Frederick Goodall, who had previously accompanied the party to Scotland, there were some lively exchanges. In his reminiscence, Goodall wrote:

After he had seen most of her studies of Highland cattle he asked, "Why don't you work in watercolors, for if you did you could, with a very fine sable brush, put in every hair in your studies." Her answer was, "I do not paint in watercolor and I could not; it would be impossible to put in every hair; even a photo could not do it." "If you come to dine with me some day," he retorted, "I will show you a watercolor drawing—made in Scotland—in which I put in every leaf of a tree in the foreground . . . !" Mr. Ruskin continued, "I do not see that you use purple in the shades." "But," she said, "I never see shade two days alike, and I never see it purple." "I always see it purple," and he emphasized it, "yes, red and blue."

At times during that first evening encounter, the conversation grew dangerously animated. Gambart remembers Ruskin's crying out, "I don't yield: to vanquish me you would have to crush me." RB answered, "I wouldn't go so far as that." After Ruskin had left, Gambart asked RB what she had thought of him. "He is a gentleman," she replied, "an educated gentleman, but he is a theorist. He sees nature with a small eye, just like a bird."

Gambart's efforts to engage Ruskin's support in the cause of RB were not entirely successful. When Ruskin published his *Academy Notes of the French Exhibition of 1857*—a work that Gambart had previously pressed him to undertake—he registered distinct reservations. Writing of a painting called *The Plow* he offered some acerbic advice:

> This lady gains in power every year, but there is one stern fact concerning art which she will do well to consider, if she means her power to reach full development. No painter of animals ever yet was entirely great who shrank from painting the human face; and Mdlle. Bonheur clearly *does* shrink from it. . . . In the *Horse Fair* the human faces were nearly all dexterously, but disagreeably, hidden, and the one chiefly shown had not the slightest character. Mdlle. Bonheur may rely upon this, that if she cannot paint a man's face, she can neither paint a horse's or a dog's nor a bull's. There is in every animal's eye a dim image and gleam of humanity, a flash of strange light through which their life looks out and up to our great mystery of command over them, and claims the fellowship of the creature, if not of the soul. I assure Mdlle. Bonheur, strange as the words may sound to her, after what she has been told by huntsmen and racers, she has never painted a horse yet. She has only painted trotting bodies of horses.

Ruskin's opinion did not waver. In 1858 he wrote a letter to his father after having read a book on horse-taming:

> Among the many things which pleased me (I shall forget to say this if I don't say it at once) was the testimony it bore to that peculiar fineness of make, and subtlety of spirit in the horse which I think Lewis has expressed so exquisitely and Rosa Bonheur missed so ignorantly. . . .

Nearly thirty years later Ruskin was still censuring Bonheur, comparing her unfavorably with Landseer and remarking that "her feelings for animals . . . were more akin to the menagerie keeper's love."

Ruskin's disapproval did not brake the enthusiasm for Bonheur's works in England. As she herself said, if ever the French tired of her work, the English would always be there to support her. She had good reason to believe it, since England was her chief source of revenue during the 1860s and 1870s. Her triumphant tour had greatly stimulated her sales. In addition, Victorian England was particularly cordial to *animaliers*, being sentimental about animals to an inordinate degree. Victoria herself led the way. When, for instance, during the Jubilee year in 1887 the Queen declared an amnesty for thousands of prisoners all over the British empire, she specifically excluded those imprisoned for cruelty to animals, which she regarded as "one of the worst traits in human nature." This was the period that saw the establishment of the Royal Society for the Prevention of Cruelty to Animals and the publication of such humane tracts as Anna Sewell's sentimental but effectively polemical novel *Black Beauty*.

In general, the British response to animal painters was rather technical in nature and decidedly influenced by the nature of the subjects. RB's specialist's eye for various species in the animal kingdom and her interest in verisimilitude were congenial to English taste. An English painter, H. W. B. Davis, writing in 1904, recalled that her reputation in England

fanned as it was by the exertions of the chief picture-dealers of the day, who had introduced her works into England, where public taste is, possibly, less discriminating, more easily led, and a keen judgment less general in matters of art than on the Continent, was immediate and possibly a little in excess of what was due.

RB took away an undying admiration for the English animal painters. Under their influence her experiment in the broad manner seen in *The Horse Fair* was abandoned. Her friend Paul Chardin pointed out in 1903 that her impressions in England were permanent. She

especially admired Landseer, whose touch is so delicate and so amorous of detail and form, and she had quite a quantity of superb engravings from the canvases of this artist, many of which were superior to the originals. In her folios were also many English engravings representing animals. . . .

at Fontainebleau

The moist perfume of English pastures and the scent of Scotland's heather had, as one of her critics put it, "impregnated" RB, to the great irritation of the French critics. After the Exposition Universelle of 1855, RB showed little inclination to show in the annual Salons, and her work did not appear again in public in Paris until 1867, when several writers took the occasion to disparage her works after *The Horse Fair*. Thoré-Burger, who had once written so enthusiastically of her pastoral landscapes, reversed himself and sarcastically referred to her as "Miss" rather than Mlle. Bonheur in his review. Probably his harshness contributed to RB's growing bitterness concerning her reception in her own country, since he was at the time one of the most important critics. His asperity sums up the criticisms that had appeared in the art journals for more than a decade and is worth recording at length for what it reveals of RB's declining status in France after 1855:

> Since her adoption by the English who have made her fortune, we have seen none of her paintings in the French exhibitions and not even in sales. At the Exposition Universelle of 1855 at Paris she had only one minor picture. This time she exhibits ten of her notable works, all belonging to the English aristocracy except the *Sheep* that the Empress of France has saved from being transported across the sea. . . . After the success of *The Horse Fair* and some other pictures that were greatly admired in England, Miss Rosa studied the works of Landseer, Ward, and other favorite painters of Britannic sport so successfully that at present she is

Château de By, near Fontainebleau. ❧ Bought in 1860 by Rosa Bonheur and Nathalie Micas, this stately manor house, parts of which date back to the fifteenth century, was to be Rosa's home until her death in 1899.

The vast country house with its acres of pastures and woodlands was also the habitat for Bonheur's ever-changing menagerie, which included at one time or another gazelles, deer, elk, mouflons, Icelandic ponies, Percherons, bulls from Falkirk, goats, and a *vache grognante de Tartarie* (yak). Crowded in the barnyards as well was an unusually wide variety of the "regulars."

like a pupil of Landseer. Her pictures have their reddish tone, undecided touch, glassy and mannered effect . . . I fear that her exhibit has not justified the happy painter's English celebrity in the estimation of French *amateurs*. . . .

While she was still in her atelier at the rue d'Assas, before she withdrew to a country estate, RB had not been totally isolated from French admirers, despite Thoré-Burger's account. There are many reports of visits to the studio, and she spoke of her Fridays, when she received the most "brilliant" company, among them members of the imperial court, newly anointed members of the peerage, and, as she often proudly reported, M. de Morny himself. She enjoyed the attention during the 1850s, but she also began to worry about the loss of working time. Toward the late 1850s she began to toy with the idea of leaving Paris, of "going back to the birds, as Aristophanes says." She and the Micas family began to scour the environs of Paris, and in the summer of 1859 they found a château in the tiny village of By on the edge of the Forest of Fontainebleau. There RB had a larger atelier constructed, and during the following summer she settled down to a life of relative seclusion.

At the time RB settled in By, it was a village of some four hundred souls on the northern edge of the forest. The château grounds, as Theodore Stanton wrote, seemed to be "cut out of the very forest itself, the trees at the end of her property and those of the contiguous forest being of the same kind. In the wall at the back of her grove is a wooden double gate which opens directly into the forest from which it is separated only by a narrow, shady lane."

Down this lane the chatelaine of By wandered almost daily. Occasionally she brought her rifle for shooting small game, a right she had won from the Emperor himself. (One of the anomalies in RB's character was her very matter-of-fact attitude toward the hunting of animals, or, according to certain of her acquaintances, her downright taste for the kill.) RB's knowledge of the 40,000-acre forest was so intimate that she knew every rock and tree and most of the cartographical names that the mapmaker C. F. Denecourt applied to various places: *la Mare aux Fées, le Long Rocher, l'Oasis de Chopin*, etc. The painter

Rear gate of the Bonheur residence. ✤ "I have spent the last three nights almost entirely in the forest," Rosa once wrote a friend. "This evening I am returning to the Mare aux Fées, where I am going to try to reproduce an admirable effect of the moon reflected in the water. You hear the owls and frogs having a concert, and then the stags come down to drink."

The courtyard at By. ❦ "With a friend of her childhood I had rung at the gate and been admitted by a black-haired maid, who barred the passage while we explained our errand," the American painter Henry Bacon wrote, describing his visit to Bonheur's studio in 1880. "As we followed her across the courtyard a young doe sprang out of our path, the dogs regarded us curiously, and the caged eagle awoke from his afternoon nap to gaze lazily at us."

Bonheur had built this picturesque brick addition to house her studio, carriage house, and coachmen's quarters.

Henri Cain recalled that "she would start out early in the morning and would stop to sketch. You couldn't get her to come to Paris if she was in the midst of a study. 'I can't leave now,' she would say to me; 'the forest is too beautiful at this moment, flaming with magnificent foliage which is so soon to fade.'" Her deep love of the allées and clearings in the forest was obvious to all who visited By. Some of her most lyrical descriptions in letters derived from her always renewed pleasure in the forest:

> Fontainebleau forest in winter is beauty in perfection, with its long avenues of pure untrodden snow, save for the small hoofs of the deer. Then there are glimpses of the stags browsing in groups, their graceful bounding away when they catch sight of you, the lovely golden sunsets seen through leafless trees, and the biting wind sweeping over all.

In later years, her neighbor M. Grivot reported, "She would start at dawn in her tilbury, attended by her faithful servant Stephen. Ensconcing herself in the wildest and most picturesque spot, she would hang her watch on a branch, place her firearm within reach, and then dismiss her servant, who came back to fetch her at the appointed time."

Life was well regulated at By by the majordomo, Mme. Micas. Both Nathalie and RB attended to the numerous animals (at one time there were as many as forty sheep), and Nathalie served as studio assistant, laying on underpaintings or tracing drawings on canvas. RB's attachment to Nathalie remained strong, although friends reported occasional rifts, probably incited by Mme. Micas. RB understood many of Nathalie's eccentricities and fondly poked fun at her. A friend recalled that RB was never taken in by the superior airs of Nathalie and "enjoyed the absurd side of her character as much as anybody else."

The "absurd" side was well documented by Paul Chardin, who spent many days at By and used to keep RB company in the evenings, smoking cigarettes and talking before the open fire. Nathalie, he said, was naturally tragic, both in her waxen-colored face and her majestic gestures. She was given to wearing flamboyant clothes and was especially fond of red and black. She generally wore hats turned up in the Spanish fashion,

Hermann Raunheim: *C. F. Denecourt.* 1858. ❧ "Next to my parents," Rosa once said, "I owe most to dear old Denecourt." This shy and eccentric little ex-sergeant spent fifty years—and 43,000 francs of his own gold—to map the tangled wildness of the vast Forest of Fontainebleau. With a pot of paint tucked under his redingote, "the Christopher Columbus of the Forest" would blaze the trees and rocks with blue so that the visitor could follow some of his 160 kilometers of private trails. He was also a special favorite of Nerval, Baudelaire, Hugo, Musset, Lamartine, and Sand.

In the 1860s, when the forest was being plundered by quarry men, woodcutters, and hunters, a petition for its conservation was drawn up by Denecourt and his friends—the artists in the surrounding villages—and sent to Napoleon III. Bonheur was an active member of this group.

trimmed with plumes that, he said, accentuated the disagreeable sallowness of her complexion. "When a dreamy fit came over her, she went to air her melancholy in a solitary walk, her head surmounted by the red and black plumed hat. It was almost impossible for a person meeting her to help bursting into laughter."

Among Nathalie's hobbies was that of playing doctor, and she served as veterinarian to the By menagerie. Her interest in science did not stop there, however. She fancied herself an inventor and spent hours fiddling with various inventions, the most extraordinary being a railroad brake guaranteed to prevent accidents. For this endeavor RB showed considerable amused indulgence and went to great lengths to further her friend's ambitions. She subsidized the building of a miniature railway on the grounds and personally approached the old Saint-Simonians now in the imperial service in the hope of finding an investor. All this took a lot of her time, and she complained to her family that she could not work and was "living like my dogs." She persisted all the same and eventually persuaded an engineer from the Paris, Lyons, and Mediterranean Railways to come and inspect Nathalie's masterpiece and report back to the government. His cool response, and the responses of others RB had tried to interest in Nathalie's invention, exasperated RB, who sometimes supported Nathalie's conviction that it was only because she was a woman that she failed. The engineer dutifully reported to the government:

> The aim of the invention is to transform, momentarily, a car into a sort of sledge by intoducing under the wheel a wedge which slips along the rail. There are eight wedges for each car, four for use when the train is moving forward and four when it is backing. I found there a little tramway about a hundred yards or more long, which began with a strong incline and ended with a level and a slight incline. The brakes were attached to the little platform cars about a yard long and two feet wide, which were several times started down the incline and stopped by means of brakes.

Unfortunately, the engineer added, the mechanism would probably not work on a real train. "Everything of this kind is easy when weight and speed do not have to be reckoned with."

Miniature of Nathalie Micas. Atelier, By. ✤ "The Great Nana of China," as Bonheur was fond of calling her beloved friend Nathalie, died in 1889 at By. "Her loss broke my heart," grieved Rosa, "and it was a long time before I found any relief in my work from this bitter ache."

The invention did provide some merriment. One afternoon when Nathalie got several women friends to mount the cars and travel down the incline, the brake either didn't work or brought the train to a sudden standstill, with the result, as Hippolyte Peyrol reported, "that these good ladies were all thrown off on the grass and into the air. Though no bones were broken, there was a conspicuous display of white undergarments."

These amusing details of Nathalie's eccentricities did not diminish RB's respect for her, nor her emotional dependency. Nathalie consoled her for the personal attacks that grew more frequent once she had left Paris for By, and she was RB's chief source of affection in later years. Her own family, still disapproving of the liaison with Nathalie, seemed to have less and less importance in her life. The depth of RB's feelings for Nathalie were revealed after Nathalie's death on June 22, 1889; RB grieved for months and found life almost unendurable. She wrote to Mme. Cain:

> . . . you can very well understand how hard it is to be separated from a friend like my Nathalie, whom I loved more and more as we advanced in life; for she had borne with me the mortifications and stupidities inflicted on us by the silly, ignorant, low-minded people. She alone knew me, and I, her only friend, knew what she was worth.

Rosa Bonheur: Sketches of Nathalie Micas' brake invention. 1863. Atelier, By. ⚜ Rosa captures with her deft hand Nathalie's impetuous embrace of her *"collaborateur en mécanique"*; also the embraces of the dogs, and of the gentlemen at left.

Rosa Bonheur est la première
femme qui a été décorée pour
son talent artistique.
En dehors du courage et du dévouement
la femme ne recevrait jamais
cette haute distinction.
Il m'est donc de me rappeler
que le 15 Juin 1865, pendant la
Régence il m'a été permis, avec

le consentement de l'Empereur,
de créer ce précédent, sous l'égide
du nom de la grande artiste

Eugénie

22 février
1902.

14.
Royal Acclaim

During her years at Fontainebleau, RB almost never consorted with fellow artists, with the exception of Chardin, whom she fondly called her *"rapin,"* while he called her "my general." He mentions that she had nothing to do with the Barbizon painters, but there he probably exaggerated. RB knew and liked her fellow animal painter Constant Troyon and was well enough acquainted with the Swiss-born Karl Bodmer to borrow studies of American Indians from him. It is probably true, however, as Chardin wrote, that "living on the opposite side of the forest, I doubt if Rosa Bonheur ever put foot in Barbizon. . . . In fact she never had many artist friends at her By home. . . ."

If few artists made their way to By, others, among them collectors, dealers, and even crowned heads, did. Even after she re-

(OPPOSITE, BELOW) Charles Maurand: *The Empress Eugénie Visiting the Rosa Bonheur Atelier*. Engraving after a sketch by Isidore Deroy. June 1865. ✠ On the last afternoon of her regency, with her husband about to return from Algeria, the Empress Eugénie hurriedly visited Rosa Bonheur's atelier to award her the Cross of the Legion of Honor. Of the many conflicting versions of this unexpected event, Rosa favored one in which the Empress—while embracing her—pinned the decoration onto her smock. It was only after Eugénie's departure that she discovered the purpose of the impromptu imperial visit.

(OPPOSITE, ABOVE) Letter signed by Eugénie regarding Rosa Bonheur's Legion of Honor award. 1902. ✠ "Rosa Bonheur was the first woman who was honored for her artistic talent. Other than for courage and for devotion, no woman had received this high distinction. I recall that on the 15th of June 1865, during the regency, I was allowed—with the approval of the Emperor—to create this precedent under the aegis of the name of this great artist."

moved herself from Paris, RB continued to attract wealthy foreigners and highly placed government officials—a fact that in spite of her Saint-Simonian formation never ceased to delight and impress her. She took pleasure in telling her biographers of the many letters she had ignored from women of high society who, influenced by the Empress, wished to visit her in By. On the other hand, whenever some high-ranking official visited, she reported the fact to her family and intimate friends, often in a self-mocking tone that only thinly concealed her evident delight. She was, of course, most excited when royalty descended at By. When the Emperor of Brazil paid his call, she wrote to her doctor:

> You will be glad to know, dear and good doctor, that I have been honored with the visit of a fine sovereign par excellence. . . . I refer to His Majesty, the Emperor of Brazil, who, as you know, is, beside his birth, a man distinguished for his learning, artistic talent, tastes, and elevated mind. You can understand what my emotions must have been on this occasion.

Bonheur's socialist background did not affect her Cinderella-like wonder that such things could happen. She persisted in trying to see in royalty the characteristics of fairy-story monarchs. Writing to another neighbor in By about the visit of the Emperor of Brazil, she asserted that "I was happy once more to meet with a proof of the great and noble simplicity of sovereigns so misunderstood by fools and ingrates."

Her reverent attitude toward royalty was shaped partially by the marked interest the Empress Eugénie took in her. The two visits of the Empress were among RB's favorite stories, and she always enjoyed recounting them in detail. The first visit occurred in 1864. Her stepbrother, Hippolyte Peyrol, happened to be visiting and he recorded the story (although somewhat differently from RB's own account): He and RB were sitting in the studio smoking their cigarettes after lunch when they heard carriage bells and the clatter of horses' hooves. RB guessed the visitor was an irritating woman who always brought with her very dull people, and she instructed Peyrol to tell the maid that she was out. He was about to leave the room when the maid burst in announcing that the Empress and her court were approaching the studio.

> When this announcement was made Rosa was attired in her blue working blouse, which she immediately started to take off. But in her haste and the excitement of the moment, she had forgotten to undo the top button and her head wouldn't go through. For an instant we both feared she might be caught in this ludicrous position by the imperial party.

RB succeeded in getting into a jacket just as the Empress entered, and she quickly recovered her composure. The Empress and her suite remained an hour, browsing among RB's drawings and looking at the paintings on the wall and easel. RB was eminently pleased with the visit, "the most gracious visit that a sovereign can pay an artist," as she wrote in a letter to her sister and brother. She mentions that the Empress commissioned a painting "in the most charming manner" and, as RB escorted her to her carriage, put out her hand, which RB thought it her duty to kiss. "Thereupon, with the greatest kindness, this sovereign, whose simplicity and affability add to her distinction, did me the honor to embrace me."

The Empress's second visit occurred almost a year later, and again there was a bit of comic confusion. This time it was Micas who was caught unprepared. "Just at the critical moment of the entrance," RB reported with amusement to Chardin, "she was taking a Barèges bath. She got out hurriedly, with a slipper on one foot and a buskin on the other, since in a case of embarrassment it is a matter of putting on whatever is handy. A white dressing-gown together with a feather-trimmed hat completed her attire in this instance!" According to another painter friend, Joseph Verdier, Nathalie never emerged from the bath; RB had locked her in, and Nathalie remained furious for years afterwards. RB also spoke of this momentous visit for years afterwards, for it was on this occasion that the Empress, taking advantage of the Emperor's absence and her temporary regency, bestowed upon Rosa the Legion of Honor, pinning the cross, which she called a "little jewel," on her best velvet jacket.

Nicaise de Keyser: *The Great Artists—the Nineteenth Century School.* Oil, 1878. Musée Cheret, Nice. ✤ Seated from left to right: J. M. W. Turner, Sir Edwin Landseer, Rosa Bonheur, J. L. E. Meissonier, Peter Cornelius, Ary Scheffer, Ingres, Horace Vernet. Standing: Hiram Powers, Millais, Alma-Tadema, J. L. Gerôme, Firth, Canova, Thorwaldsen, Leys, Delacroix, Delaroche, Gallait, de Keyser himself, H. Makart, and J. N. Robert-Fleury. This huge painting was one of a set of four commissioned by Ernest Gambart from de Keyser, a Belgian painter of historical subjects and the Director of the Antwerp Academy from 1855 to 1879.

The true climax of the visit was the Empress's invitation to lunch with her and the Emperor at Fontainebleau. RB was thrilled with the invitation and not a little intimidated. The court that the Empress had so laboriously established was expected to take part in full Second Empire regalia, even at luncheons. Memoirs of the period frequently allude to Eugénie's exaggerated notions of courtly protocol and the dull pomp of court gatherings. Eugénie, it seems, could not forget her childhood obsession with Marie Antoinette, and in her imperious way she tried without much success to make her *haut-bourgeois* courtiers over into Louis Seize models. Luncheon at Fontainebleau was therefore formal, and RB had to ask for, and was granted, special permission not to wear *décolletage*.

This occasion caused RB a great deal of anxiety. Her lack of education and her unpolished manners secretly embarrassed her. She did wear unconventional dress, smoke cigarettes, and in general comport herself defiantly, but underneath, she was not comfortable with the role of social rebel. Her uneasiness about the visit to Fontainebleau is apparent in her lengthy accounts of the visit, in which she alternates between a tone of exultant professional pride and modest, almost childish, anxiety about doing the right thing. She was especially unnerved by the sophisticated Princesse Metternich, who, she felt, watched her condescendingly, "no doubt expecting that I should break the rules of etiquette."

The tremulous emotions of that August day still animated RB's accounts at the end of her life. She described her dress—velvet jacket with gold buttons and a straight black skirt—as probably offering an amusing contrast with the enormous crinolines of the other ladies. The Empress sent an elegant carriage, which deposited her at the foot of the grand staircase of the château. There, however, she was turned back by a guard who said that only the Emperor and Empress used that entry. When RB went to the other door, she was sent back to the first again. After this, she said, she had a strong desire to return home. But happily the first guard took another look at her invitation and allowed her to enter the château through an aisle of halberdiers. Once she was inside, RB's discomfort became acute:

> At the moment I entered the salon François Ier, Mme. de Metternich herself was there in a deep conversation with some young people. None of them seemed to notice my presence, and seeing that, I installed myself quietly in one of the large armchairs near the chimney. I knew that at the court the general humor was a bit mocking, especially in the circle of the celebrated ambassador's wife, and my greatest wish, for that moment, was not to make too great a fault in etiquette that could make them laugh at my expense. Then one of the young people, suddenly leaving the little group around the ambassador's wife, approached me and bowed.
> "Mlle. Rosa Bonheur?" he inquired.
> "Yes, monsieur."

Music score by Georges Bizet. 1867. Atelier, By. ✣ "I would also like to divulge to you some verse," Rosa wrote to "Friend Mène" about a song Bizet had composed in her honor at the time of her Legion of Honor award, "so neatly inspired by your kind friendship for Mlle. Bonheur and put to charming music by M. Bizet, the composer, whose acquaintance I had the pleasure of making. . . ." The lyrics of this song were written by Auguste Cain, the animal sculptor.

"Our Rosa was never coquettish,
Interested herself not with flowers or ribbons.
The Empress wanted her dress
To have one, and of the most magnificent kind. . . ."

Napoleon III. ❀ "A seat near the Emperor was offered me at the table," remembered Rosa of the day she spent at the Château at Fontainebleau, "and as long as lunch lasted he talked with me about the intelligence of animals. After lunch, the Empress took me into her gondola on the lake...."

"The Emperor will be coming in a moment, mademoiselle. Perhaps you don't know, never having been at court, that when Their Majesties enter the room the custom is not to rise until their signal. I think I should warn you."

The trap was obvious to me, and I answered in a sharp tone: "It is true that I have never lived at court like you, monsieur, but all the same I will not await the signal and will rise immediately."

A little discountenanced, this young man so eager to instruct me rejoined Mme. de Metternich's group, and I observed with satisfaction that certain little mocking smiles immediately ceased.

At last the door opened. The Emperor and Empress made their entrance followed by the general who had invited me, and who, according to my meager notion of courtly procedures, was intended to serve as my escort. Contrary to what they had so eagerly told me, all the people in the salon rose, and my young man quicker than any.

They presented me. To my great confusion, it was the Emperor himself who offered me his arm to conduct me to the table, where he seated me at his right. During the whole meal he never ceased to talk to me and give me his attention.

RB continues, mentioning that the menu was of course choice, but that even at the table of an emperor one doesn't always find fresh eggs. After lunch the Empress invited RB for a ride in her gondola, where she took the oars herself. The day concluded with RB's invitation to the Prince Royal to visit her menagerie.

What lingered in RB's memory was the affront to her dignity, for which she felt Mme. de Metternich responsible. When the ambassadress later wrote asking permission to visit By, RB did not respond. Not to be put off, the ambassadress arrived unannounced one day, surrounded by young courtiers. RB flung open the double doors of the château and planted herself on the doorsill. Mme. de Metternich commented that RB opened both doors as if she, the ambassadress, were the Empress herself. RB answered sarcastically that she had only opened both doors in order to permit the ambassadress's exaggerated crinoline to pass through. The visit did not go well. Mme. de Metternich spied a drawing she liked and asked RB if she could have it in exchange for some of her best vintage wines. RB thanked her in a very dry tone and informed her that she never made exchanges or sales at By. The ambassadress would have to apply to Messrs. Gambart and Tedesco, who were her intermediaries. At this Mme. de Metternich was "a little vexed" and never again repeated her visit.

RB's response to Mme. de Metternich and other of the more sophisticated members of the court was that of a wary schoolgirl. The ambassadress's reputation at court was well known. She was considered clever and original, with a flair that put the dowdy members of Eugénie's entourage in the shadows. Not beautiful—she called herself *singe* [monkey] *à la mode*—she nonetheless attracted men, and they crowded her Thursdays, which sometimes ended with the hostess smoking with the men and entertaining them with risqué music-hall songs. Prosper Merimée, the loyal poet of the Empire, called her "quite an odd mixture of *lorette* [prostitute] and *grande dame*." Despite her reputation for jest and levity, Mme. de Metternich took a serious interest in the arts, particularly music. She was largely responsible, for instance, for bringing the first performance of Wagner's *Tannhäuser* to Paris in 1861. RB's negative judgment was probably based as much on the unkind gossip that circulated about the ambassadress as it was on her own encounter. Rosa was naïve and tended to think that those of the entourage, above all the Empress herself, who treated her with deference and kindness were in fact kind and good. Her judgment of the half-brother of the Emperor, the Duc de Morny, was particularly naïve. Although he was elegant, breezy, and a dandy, he was hardly the born gentleman that RB assumed. His ruthless business practices won him an ugly reputation, and he was greatly resented. Victor Hugo in *L'Histoire d'un Crime* characterized him angrily:

He combined a certain liberty of ideas with a readiness to accept useful crimes; was dissipated, yet well concentrated; ugly, good-humored, ferocious, well-dressed, fearless; willing to leave under lock and key a brother in prison but willing to risk his head for a brother on the throne; conscienceless, irreproachably elegant, infamous, and amiable—at need a perfect Duke.

15.
Politics and Personality

Safe-conduct pass issued to Rosa Bonheur by the Commander of the Prussian Army in France on September 26, 1870. ❦ Wanting no special favors from the enemy, Rosa was outraged by this document. It was reported that she immediately tore it to bits in the face of his officers, but the document still exists.

RB's loyalty to the Empress never faltered. When the Franco-Prussian war of 1870 erupted, she genuinely feared for the fate of the Imperial couple. Her conversion from the Saint-Simonian doctrine was nearly complete. After the declaration of the Third Republic, she wrote to Chardin, "I can no more swallow this cardboard republic than I could the earlier one of 1848, especially as I now have the discernment that comes with age together with its real, honest independence." RB's age was not yet very advanced—she was forty-eight—but she often spoke of herself as settled into a permanent wisdom concerning the perfidies of the world of men. The turmoil of the war invigorated her, however, and brought out her schoolgirl ambitions to wield the sword. In letters she wrote of her "métier of regional Amphytrion" and in conversation spoke with zest of her military adventures. Numerous accounts by friends and neighbors attest to RB's simple and energetic response to the Prussian invasion. The town nearest By, Thoméry, was a kind of headquarters for the alarmed citizens in 1870. One of its residents recalled RB's initial response:

. . . my father, a retired captain of the army, organized among the older inhabitants a sort of home guard. RB joined the company, and more than once did I see her at that time, with her gun over her shoulder, march and drill with her male neighbors. Of course her men's clothes made this all the easier and more natural.

The role of warrior definitely appealed to RB. Once she tried to incite her neighbors to make a stand to hold the Prussians off from crossing the Seine at By. They wisely refused, pointing out that the Prussians would burn the village in retaliation. She did manage to induce one neighbor to station himself with her on the banks of the Seine, where they spent most of the night firing at the enemy's sentinel across the river. When finally the Prussians did occupy Thoméry, taking several prominent citizens hostage, she showed courageous defiance. She had worked out an elaborate plan that if worse came to worst, she would first paint her animals, then eat them, rather than let them fall into the hands of the enemy. She even debated burning down her château. Eventually, however, there were Prussian officers billeted in her château. Her cook reported that she steadfastly refused to dine with them and never permitted them in her studio. One of her closest friends, Consuelo Fould, maintained that Prince Frederick Charles had sent RB a safe-conduct, "but she, indignant that she could be supposed capable of accepting a favor from an enemy of France, tore up the paper in the presence of the officer who bore it, and informed him that she felt in honor bound not to allow herself to be treated any better than the humblest peasant in the village." This account is somewhat romanticized, however—the safe-conduct document still exists. But it is certainly true that RB stoutly displayed her contempt for the Prussian officers on more than one occasion. It was almost a game for her at times, and she took childish delight when her favorite old reindeer splashed mud on one of the officers. The mayor of Thoméry was worried about RB's behavior and told her to restrain herself as she was no Jeanne d'Arc.

RB's growing conservatism, both as an artist and as a citizen, is seen in her loyalty to the Empire and her newfound distaste for republican government. She loathed the events following the siege of Paris. The Commune, in her view, was an unparalleled disaster. In May 1871 she wrote irritatedly to Mme. Mène:

What the deuce can you be doing in the Paris of Father Duchesne? Can it be that you are mixed up in the Commune, my old Mène? I can't swallow that even if you told me so. I don't suppose

Rosa Bonheur: Sketch of Prussian soldiers. Atelier, By.
". . . And if the Uhlans come," Rosa wrote her brother Auguste in 1870 as the Prussians were advancing toward her village, "I'll ask them if they don't want their portraits painted to send to their wives and mothers, since I hope not many of the poor devils will return to their homes."

Rosa Bonheur's unfinished sketch of deer in the Atelier, By (81 × 65.5 cm.). ❧ "I am going to try and send you a haunch of deer, which will be a feast for you," Rosa wrote her sister during the grim winter of the Prussian occupation. "For three days before the deer was killed I was making sketches of him. The piece that I dined on was excellent, splendid meat and covered with fat."

Nathalie Micas and Rosa Bonheur at Nice. Ca. 1882. ✤ For this photograph the women wore sedate black costumes; the only ornaments are Bonheur's honorary medals and the necklace on Nathalie's dog.

you are a partisan of the artistic principles of Citizen Courbet, who has some talent for knife painting but whom I find heavy in every other respect. . . .

Later, she was somewhat reconciled when many of her old friends from imperial days managed to be incorporated in the new Republic. She especially liked President Carnot, whose father had been with her own in the convent of Ménilmontant, and who had once spoken to her warmly about the rights of women. When he was assassinated in 1894 she was deeply distressed:

This new atrocity turned me for a time to historical and political questions. I reread the writing of Maxime du Camp on the scenes that accompanied our last social battle, the bloody days of the Commune. All these crimes show, alas, that the aftermath of a war can, sometimes be worse than the war itself.

After some reflection, RB came to attribute part of the blame on science, which always finds new means of destruction. A lingering Saint-Simonian sentiment of her youth resurfaced and she wrote:

Ah! If nations could only agree to employ their resources to perfect agriculture and improve transportation, and to bring all their girl children a good education, what an explosion of happiness there would be on earth!

Her general disillusionment and her final conviction that royalty makes for the best political arrangement is seen in a letter she wrote in February 1894. She had spent a long night nursing a sick puppy:

Here you have one of the results of being a great artist who cares nothing about the grandeurs of this world and who finds, unfortunately, that the human race generally is not worth as much as the dumb animals. If we did not have good friends here below, it would be a real bit of good fortune never to have to come on this earth, where, by the way, a people find amusement in watching the procession of the queen of the washerwomen after having cut off the head of the true queen!

The reference to both Marie Antoinette and her admirer, the deposed Eugénie, was prompted by the Nice Mardi Gras celebration in which a young washerwoman, elected by other washerwomen, is crowned each year. RB spent much time in Nice after the Franco-Prussian war. Gambart at first had graciously put his villa at her disposal, but later RB constructed her own. She and Nathalie sallied forth fairly often to attend regal receptions at Gambart's residence. RB fully accepted this elaborate society. On official occasions she would wear all her decorations, and once, she wrote to her sister, having left some behind, she had to borrow M. Gambart's.

RB's work took a slight turn after the Franco-Prussian war. During the 1860s she worked assiduously to provide Gambart with portraits of deer, reindeer, horses, and dogs, all creatures who roamed her own preserve. After the war she became intensely interested in studying felines, much as had Géricault during his English sojourn. She began to frequent the zoological gardens to sketch lions, tigers, and panthers. In 1873 she was invited by the director of the Cirque d'Hiver to make studies of a favorite lioness. Always alert to RB's needs, Gambart arranged in 1880 to have two lions delivered to By. The male soon died, but the female lingered. RB said, "She was tender and faithful as a dog. Sometimes she would stand on her hind legs and put her front paws on my shoulders in order to caress me more easily." The lioness also died after a poignant scene in which the sick animal attempted to climb up the stairs in the château to find RB. Her old lion Nero, whom she used to let roam freely in the courtyard and who used to peer over the fence, frightening passersby, eventually had to be given to the zoo, but her little favorite, Fathma, whom she acquired in 1885, remained healthy and provided RB with a model for many sketches during the last years of the artist's life. In these drawings RB tried to capture her vision of the nobility of wild animals and sometimes seemed to retrieve—at least in the incidental sketches— the broad manner she had briefly adopted during her work on *The Horse Fair*.

RB's attitude toward her animal subjects never changed. As a professional *animalier*, she shared the naturalist's view, always intent on rendering physiological details correctly and wary of anthropomorphizing. But as an animal lover, she had more complex views that mitigated her approach to her work. When the popular novelist and man of letters Jules Claretie visited her at By, she declared to him that Descartes had calumniated animals and that only La Fontaine had understood them. She told him: "To conquer them one must love them. These beasts are formidable only when they are feared or when we hurt them."

RB was not alone in her tacit assumption that animals possessed individual characters, or even souls. (Of her dying lion-

(RIGHT) Rosa Bonheur: *Studies of of Lioness* (detail). Pencil. Klumpke. ❧ "The eye—is it not the mirror of the soul in all living creatures," Rosa told her protégée Anna Klumpke when discussing some of her art theories with her. (BELOW) Rosa Bonheur: *Studies of Fathma.* Oil, ca. 1885. Collection Mr. and Mrs. Harold F. Mueller (48½ × 64 cm). (OPPOSITE, ABOVE) Bonheur and Fathma in By. Ca. 1885. ❧ "Fathma," Rosa told Klumpke, "was more gentle and affectionate than Pierette [her first lioness], following me everywhere like a poodle . . . and she would run freely into my bedroom, often enough turning it into a shambles." (OPPOSITE, BELOW) Rosa Bonheur: *Royalty at Home.* Watercolor, 1885. Minneapolis Institute of Arts (39.4 × 55.9 cm).

ess she said, "My lioness loved, therefore she had more soul than certain people who do not love.") After the great debate between Cuvier and Geoffroy de Saint-Hilaire, there were many voices raised to combat the Cartesian position. Jules Michelet, one of Louis Napoleon's early victims, stated their views unequivocally in his curious book *The Bird* published in 1856: "Preconceived ideas and dogmatic theories apart, you cannot offend God by restoring a soul to the beast. How much grander is his work if he has created persons, souls, and wills than if he had constructed machines."

RB had kept many birds since her childhood and refused to see them as the "constructed machines" Descartes suggested all animals were. She stated emphatically that birds did have souls, and suggested that they might once have been human souls and had preserved their feelings despite the metamorphosis. Many artists and writers tended to believe in the transmigration of animal to human souls during the period, and RB was no exception. Geoffroy de Saint-Hilaire's arguments lent support to the romantics who wished to believe in the unity of all creation and, in some cases, went so far as to extend spiritual resemblances as well as physical between animals and humans. The use of such an analogical approach to the animal and human kingdoms was widespread.

When Roger-Milès asked RB if she had reflected on the souls of animals, she answered, "Yes, nothing is more interesting; and what must be said is that if we don't always understand animals, they always understand us." He points out that she was an assiduous reader of La Fontaine, Buffon, and Le Brun, who had been among the first to call attention to physiological similarities between beasts and men. The seventeenth-century artist Charles Le Brun had executed a series of plates comparing human and animal physiognomies. These drawings were reproduced by an author well-known to RB's circle, the Swiss physiologist Johann Kasper Lavater. In his book *The Art of Knowing Men by Their Physiognomies*, published in 1820, Lavater had explored many physical types and had carefully presented Le Brun's theories. Many artists, among them Goya, had taken a keen interest in Lavater's theories, and through him, those of his predecessor Le Brun.

(ABOVE) A life mask of Beethoven, an armoire full of glass photographic plates, and an eighteenth-century mannequin reflect some of Bonheur's interests.

(OPPOSITE) Library in the Rosa Bonheur atelier. ❧ "My sole consolation has been to read the memoirs of Dumas Père, ten volumes running," Rosa wrote Georges Cain, Curator of the Carnavalet Museum, from her sickbed. "What a braggart he is! But what a big heart he has. . . ." Her other favorites were Sir Walter Scott, James Fenimore Cooper, La Fontaine, Buffon, Le Brun, Eugène Sue, George Sand, and Cervantes.

Rosa Bonheur: (ABOVE) *Head of Dog.* Charcoal, 1869. Musée des Beaux-Arts, Bordeaux (53 × 42 cm). ✤ (BELOW) *Head of Dog.* Charcoal and chalk, 1869. Musée des Beaux-Arts, Bordeaux (53 × 42 cm).

(OPPOSITE) Rosa Bonheur: *The Wounded Eagle.* Oil, ca. 1870. Los Angeles County Museum of Art; gift of Mrs. Justin Dart (148 × 115 cm). ✤ Bonheur did a number of paintings on this theme, such as *The Wounded Chamois* and *The Wounded Roebuck.*

RB was a close reader of Buffon. She once told Roger-Milès that she never painted the face of a fox without thinking of Buffon's admirable description of its "nature and instinct—or, if you prefer, its soul." He remarked that RB was not hampered by the literal meaning of words and made no attempt to decide whether an animal has a soul or merely instinct. What she did was to make use of her powers of observation. "Between her and the animals which she studied, looks had been exchanged. . . ."

Curiously, her powers of observation faltered before the human physiognomy, as Ruskin had noted. Whenever the human figure appears in her works, it is usually awkward, and out of proportion in relation to animals. This was true in her masterpiece, *The Horse Fair,* and was noticed even by her most sympathetic critics. Still, in some of her sketches she proved that she was an able and correct draftsman and could, on occasion, present the human figure very accurately. Professor Albert Boime concludes from this that her problem was not one of skill but a psychological failing: she simply could not allow the human to supersede her real love, which was the character of individual animals.

Most of her friends agreed that her favorite animal was the horse. Thoroughbreds, however, were not to her taste. She advised Paul Chardin not to bother with "old race-hacks who are always on wires with their greyhound legs and body," but to get a good Norman half-blood. "Man is not built for riding on greyhounds, but rather on horses that are shaped in proper proportion, supple in their movements, graceful under the bridle, and without any daredeviltry." A note found in RB's papers after her death indicates her high opinion of the horse when compared with the human animal:

The horse is, like man, the most beautiful and the most miserable of creatures, only, in the case of man, it is vice or poverty that makes him ugly. He is almost responsible for his decadence, while the horse is only a slave that the Creator has given to man, who abuses it out of his ingratitude and his worldly and egoistic poverty, until he becomes lower than the animal itself.

As this passage indicates, RB grew increasingly misanthropic as she aged. She repeatedly justified her involvement with ani-

(RIGHT) The big curling letters RB etched in blue glass decorate the skylight in Bonheur's atelier.

(BELOW) "The horse is, like man, the most beautiful and the most miserable of creatures," wrote Bonheur. Rosa painted over a dozen portraits of this Arabian, her favorite horse and model, during its lifetime. Note the RB initials used as a decorative pattern over the doorway and mantelpiece.

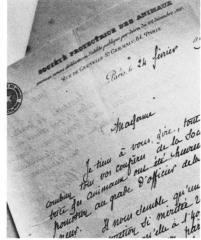

(ABOVE) Letter from the Société Protectrice des Animaux. February 24, 1894. ❧ Bonheur was an active member of the society and gave generously to its support.

(LEFT) Rosa Bonheur: *Cartload of Stones.* Drawing, ca. 1850. Atelier, By. ❧ The abuse of animals concerned Bonheur greatly; she made a number of sketches of scenes like this one, although she rarely worked them into finished paintings.

mals by pointing out how miserable the human race was, and how unreliable. Numerous letters in later years describe her pet dogs Daisy and Charlie and her various horses as her true companions. In these letters there is often an extensive vocabulary of animal similes. In fact, animal imagery in her writing became in itself a mode of expression supplementing her studio efforts. She once wrote to a former pupil referring to her as a "poor little bird who ought to have been born in swan's down." In another letter she calls her "my poor little wren," admonishing her not to work too hard as "you are as big as a mouse, as fat as a match, and as brave as a hare." To the same student and many others she referred to herself as "an old owl," or she would tell friends that "I live like my dogs" or that she was really "an old tortoise." The depth of RB's identification with animals cannot be overestimated. A deep psychological need insistently forced her to establish close relationships with her pets, whose fond gazes compensated her for her apparent sense of failure with human relationships.

16.
Buffalo Bill
and *les Peaux Rouges*

National Register of Norman Horses. Published in Quincy, Illinois, 1883. ✤ The Percheron Horse Society of America was founded by "earnest practical men determined to provide through their Association for the proper register of the Norman Horse (Percheron, Picardy and Boulonnais) in America." On the gold-embossed cover of the publication, the Association featured the head of one of the prancing Percherons from *The Horse Fair.* The four mares listed as No. 1822 to No. 1824 in the register are aptly named Rosa Bonheur.

A great event in Rosa Bonheur's later years was her encounter with Buffalo Bill Cody. She had long followed in the French tradition—from Chateaubriand with his idealization of the noble savage through Baudelaire who was entranced with George Catlin's paintings—and was full of curiosity about the American Indian. Long before Colonel Cody, known as Buffalo Bill, paid her a call at Fontainebleau in 1889, RB had collected prints and photographs of the Wild West and its animal and human denizens. She was, like her father, something of an Americanophile. She identified America with the liberation of women and with a progressive attitude that conformed to the Saint-Simonian principles of her youth. "If America marches at the forefront of modern civilization," she said, "it is because of their admirably intelligent manner of bringing up their daughters and the respect they have for their women." She often spoke of her esteem for America and sometimes compared herself to Louis Agassiz, "that glorious French zoologist, naturalized American." (He was Swiss, but French to RB.) Moreover, she had other good reasons to harbor warm feelings for America. Since 1858 when *The Horse Fair* had begun its tour of the United States, RB had been extraordinarily successful with American buyers and was predisposed in their favor.

The son of Pierre Leroux, her father's old friend, had founded the Société Hippique Percheronne in 1883 to further the fortunes of the Percheron breed. He had called upon RB, and she enthusiastically supported the society. When it published its

(LEFT) Rosa Bonheur: *Cowboy*. Pencil, ca. 1889. Atelier, By.

(RIGHT) Newspaper clippings of Buffalo Bill's visit to Rosa Bonheur's studio. September 1889. ✤ "While in the vicinity of Paris [for the Exposition Universelle of 1889] I accepted an invitation from Rosa Bonheur to visit her superb château," Buffalo Bill Cody wrote in his autobiography. Shortly afterward the local newspapers reported the eventful day the Colonel sent her his two most seasoned cowboys to tame her "*chevaux sauvages.*" The two mustangs had been a gift from John Arbuckle, a wealthy New York coffee merchant, who had shipped them to Rosa from his cattle ranch north of Cheyenne, Wyoming, a few years earlier. To the amazement of all the locals, Apache and Clair de Lune were speedily saddled and bridled by the two cowhands and were last seen being ridden into the horse car of a train bound for Paris to join the touring Buffalo Bill's Wild West Show.

Malgré les élections il y avait foule dimanche dernier aux arènes de Buffalo-Bill.

Le colonel Cody est allé hier matin rendre visite à Mlle Rosa Bonheur à Thomery. Le grand peintre met en ce moment la dernière main à une toile ou elle a représenté les chevaux et les personnages du campement indien.

—, Rosa Bonheur passe, depuis quelques jours toutes ses matinées au campement de Buffalo Bill. La grande artiste prépare un mense tableau qui est d'ores et déjà acheté le correspondant, à New-York, de la m̄ Boussod et Valadon.

Puisque nous parlons de Buffalo-Bill, que les recettes des trois derniers jour supérieures à celles des trois jours e suivi l'inauguration. N'est-ce pas preuve bien coucluante de la vogue croissante de cette exhibition.

— Certaines personnes nous dem malgré l'affluence du public, elles pe sûres de revenir sous difficultés, le arènes de Buffalo-Bill. « Les voitur être rar à cette extrémité de Pari vent-elles

Rassurons ces lecteurs. Les mo

CHRONIQUE LOCALE

Buffalo Bill's, le directeur du campement indien installé à Paris, dont tout le monde a entendu parler et a vu les exercices, est venu mardi matin à Fontainebleau. Le but de sa visite était le cottage de M̄ Rosa Bonheur, à By, près Thomery. On sait que l'illustre peintre animalier a reçu autrefois plusieurs chevaux sauvages d'Amérique; nous en avons parlé à l'époque.

Depuis l'arrivée de Buffalo Bill's à Paris, M̄ Bonheur a reçu d'important tableau dont le sujet était dès chevaux et des personnages de la troupe du colonel Cody. Elle se mit aussitôt au travail et fit plusieurs séances dans le campement indien. Pour rendre au peintre estimé la visite qui lui avait été faite, le colonel Cody est venu mardi matin chez M̄ Rosa Bonheur, à By; cette dernière l'a reconduit ensuite à Fontainebleau, où ils ont déjeuné à l'hôtel de France, et à onze heures Buffalo Bill's regagnait Paris, pour prendre part à la représentation diurne de sa troupe.

* *

Le grand peintre Rosa Bonheur avait amené d'Amérique deux Bronchos de toute beauté, que personne n'avait pu monter jusqu'ici, malgré les bons soins et les diverses méthodes du dressage. La célèbre artiste les offrit dernièrement au colonel Cody, et déjà Mexicains et cowboys, ont merveilleusement dompté ces belles bêtes.

Puisque nous parlons de *Buffalo-Bill*, disons qu'à la représentation d'hier on remarquait la présence du duc de Montmorency, de Desclauzas, de plusieurs cheiks arabes, des bog-pipers et des highlanders du colonel David White.

Saint-Potin.

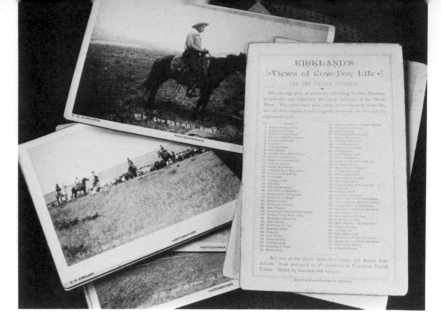

Soon after his visit to Rosa Bonheur's studio in 1889, John Arbuckle, an American admirer, sent her these photographs by C. D. Kirkland "relating to the life of the cowboys" from his cattle ranch in Wyoming. Bonheur often worked from photographs. "When one paints history," she would say, "one must be accurate. And I do not hesitate before any obstacle in obtaining the documents which I may need."

first Stud Book in 1885, she provided the frontispiece. After the book appeared in America several American horse breeders wrote to her, including John Arbuckle, president of the Royal Horse Association. She made a series of studies of stallions for the company, and as a gift he sent her some wild mustangs. Only one of the horses had been broken, and the others would return to the stables only if he led them. Eventually, two of the mustangs had to be lassoed by Buffalo Bill's cowboys and brought back to the Wild Western fold.

Although none of RB's biographers mention the sensational appearance of George Catlin with his troupe of "wild" Indians in Paris in 1845—the year RB won her first medal—it is inconceivable that she had missed the event. It was something *le tout Paris* talked about, and Catlin had also been praised in the press for his contribution to the same annual Salon in which RB had won her medal. At some point RB had acquired one of his elaborate sets of colored prints, and she had discussed him with various acquaintances. In her last years she carefully copied a number of his Indian scenes and portraits.

Since the Paris papers were filled with accounts of Catlin's stay in Paris, and such notables as George Sand, Victor Hugo, and Eugène Delacroix were enthusiasts, it is probable that RB conceived her taste for Wild West fantasies during the exciting summer and fall of 1845. The American painter had earlier made a stand in London, where he had arrived originally in 1838 with 507 paintings, 310 of them portraits of Indians. He also brought artifacts and a full-scale Crow Indian tepee with twenty-five buffalo skins covering it. He stayed in England for five years, where he produced a lithographic album of twenty-five plates in 1844 called *Catlin's North American Indian Portfolio.* RB owned one of the many subsequent editions.

After an appearance at Buckingham Palace and countless invitations to lecture and present his works and his live Indians, Catlin finally wore out his welcome and and set off for Paris. In the spring of 1845 posters, flyers, and press notices appeared announcing that Catlin's troupe of Iowa Indians would perform native songs and dances in a former dance hall that would also serve as a gallery for his paintings. A skillful showman, he piqued the curiosity of the Parisians by smuggling his Indians into the Hôtel Victoire by night and keeping them sequestered until the great day. But they were not totally sequestered; he did dress them once in full regalia and had them driven through the streets of Paris to the American embassy, setting off a long journalistic orgy of anecdotes surrounding Catlin's almost year-long run.

Interest in Catlin's Indian show ran high among artists. Delacroix commented on the "new savages" and admired their dances, comparing them to ancient Greeks, and the chief "brandishing his lance" to Ajax defying the gods. He made many sketches of Iowas, and even a poster for Catlin. Delacroix's admirer, the young poet Baudelaire, was among the rare spectators who saw not only the live Indians but also the vividness of Catlin's work. Calling him the "impresario of the Redskins," Baudelaire wrote in his Salon review of 1846:

When M. Catlin came to Paris, with his Museum and his Ioways, the word went around that he was a good fellow who could neither paint nor draw, and that if he had produced some tolerable studies, it was thanks only to his courage and his patience. Was this an innocent trick of M. Catlin, or a blunder on the part of the journalists? . . .

M. Catlin has captured the proud, free character and the noble expression of these splendid fellows in a masterly way; the structure of their heads is wonderfully understood. With their fine attitude and their ease of movement, these savages make antique sculpture comprehensible. Turning to his color, I find in it an element of mystery which delights me more than I can say. Red, the color of blood, the color of life, flowed so abundantly in his gloomy Museum that it was like an intoxication; and the landscapes—wooded mountains, vast savannahs, deserted rivers—were monotonously, eternally green.

Years later in his Salon review of 1859, Baudelaire again praised "the natural charm, so simply expressed, of Catlin's prairies and savannahs." Catlin apparently was not impressed with the poet's praise, if he knew of it at all, and instead reproduced in his publicity brochures the banalities of the local press that praised his scrupulous exactitude and described him as an intrepid traveler.

Catlin's advent in Paris spurred RB's interest in the Wild West, and her excitement reached its climax decades later with the second invasion of Indians under a new impresario, Buffalo Bill. While RB was dictating her memoirs to her protégée, Anna Klumpke, she was reminded of Buffalo Bill when she showed Klumpke a large volume of engraved plates representing Indians. "This is the work of Catlin. What wonders he could draw from the spectacle before his eyes. I worked a little like him, thanks to Colonel Cody during the Paris exposition."

Buffalo Bill produced even more of a sensation than Catlin and managed to occupy the columns of the entire French press for months. His entrepreneurial career in the United States had prepared him well even for the sophisticated city of Paris. This former scout of rather humble origins, once described by the commander of a Sioux raid in 1869 as "modest and unassuming . . . a natural gentleman in his manners, as well as in character . . . and none of the roughness of the typical frontiersman," proved to be a born showman. His exposure to the great of the world had begun while he was still a frontiersman and took prominent sportsmen and celebrities out on buffalo hunts. James Gordon Bennett of *The New York Herald*, who had been among them, returned with a sheaf of stories about the *"beau ideal* of the plains." Another was the Russian Grand Duke Alexis, who came in 1872 with droves of journalists and greatly impressed Buffalo Bill. That same year Cody made his debut as

George Catlin's Indian gallery in the Louvre. 1845. ⚜ When Louis-Philippe came to visit Catlin's Indian Gallery at the Louvre, the artist wrote in his journal that the King of France was delighted: " 'Tell these good fellows I am glad to see them, that I have been in many of the wigwams in America, when I was a young man, and they treated me everywhere kindly.' "

an actor in New York, where he was properly panned by the critics but widely acclaimed by the public. The taste of theater agreed with him, and a year later he organized his own show, getting another famed frontiersman, Wild Bill Hickock, to join him. In 1883 he organized a huge rodeolike show which he called "The Wild West, Rocky Mountain and Prairie Exhibition." The spectacle included bronco busting, trick riding, and roping displays as well as a mock battle between the Indians and the scouts. Mark Twain saw the show in 1886 and wrote Cody that he found it all perfectly genuine, "wholly free from sham and insincerity, and the effect it produced upon me by its spectacles are identical with those wrought upon me a long time ago on the frontier." Mark Twain then counseled him to take his Wild West show to England, and Colonel Cody took his advice in 1887.

In England he followed in Catlin's footsteps, engaging the interest of Queen Victoria, who sent a special messenger to the fairgrounds requesting a private showing. She came with several crowned heads and princes. Buffalo Bill induced three kings and a prince to ride in his famous Deadwood Coach and had them furiously chased by Indians. His triumph in England complete, Buffalo Bill packed up his Indians, stagecoach, horses, and

(LEFT) George Catlin: Self-portrait sketch of the making of Mah-to-toh-pa's portrait. Pen and ink, ca. 1832–1836. Collection Thomas Gilcrease Institute of American History and Art, Tulsa, Oklahoma.

(RIGHT) Rosa Bonheur: *Mandan Village—Upper Missouri.* Watercolor, 1896. Knoedler, New York. ✤ Catlin's *North American Indian Portfolio of Hunting Scenes and Amusements* was part of Bonheur's library. She made a number of copies from it.

tepees and returned home for another big season of touring. But by the following year he was ready for another rousing trans-Atlantic success. On April 28, 1889, the *New York Sun* reported the following news:

Buffalo Bill, otherwise Col. and Hon. W. F. Cody, sailed for Paris yesterday on the steamship "Persian Monarch" at the head of the Wild West show, with which he expects to surprise and delight, not only the Parisians, but all those who attend the French Exposition. His company includes 115 Indians, counting squaws and papooses, forty-eight cowboys, of whom sixteen are musicians, the rest being riders; half a dozen pretty women who can ride or shoot, as many Mexican vaqueros, not to speak of his aides, property men, camp officers, &c. His accompanying menagerie consists of twenty buffaloes, twenty-five mustangs, eight Esquimaux dogs, and 186 horses.

Rosa Bonheur: *"Buffalo Bill" Cody.* Oil, 1889. Whitney Gallery of Western
Art, Cody, Wyoming (36 × 46 cm).

These Sioux beaded buckskin shirt and leggings, silver conch belt, moccasins, and Osage bow and arrows were given to Bonheur by Buffalo Bill soon after his visit to her studio.

They were the only passengers and cargo on board.

He set up camp on a thirty-acre field opposite the Exposition grounds. On May 18 some twenty thousand people attended the premiere, including the President of the Republic, Carnot, and Queen Isabella of Spain.

The encampment of Indians enthralled the Parisians, who flocked to the grounds to observe the picturesque savages. They were amply rewarded. As a news account of October 24 told it, the citizens of Paris could in one hour transport themselves to the prairies of the Far West, then to Canada, and wind up in Mexico (Buffalo Bill had added Mexican *vaqueros* and dressage riders to his troupe before leaving America). And, the newspaper added, if the visitors were gracious enough to offer a few cigarettes to the Creeks, they could even smoke a peace pipe "with the possessors of hundreds of scalps." A provincial newspaper spoke even more enthusiastically of the event, coming up with the story that the great attraction of the Exposition—Buffalo Bill and his Indians—was a boon to science. It had been discovered, this newspaper gravely reported, that Indians possess a "special magnetic fluid" which had already cured several visitors of their ills. Still other accounts go into detail, describing such events as Annie Oakley's shooting matches and Buffalo Bill's astounding reenactment of his duel, thirteen years before, with Chief Yellow Hand of the Cheyennes, whom he had vanquished and then scalped.

Rosa Bonheur was not the only artist who haunted the fairgrounds during the seven months the troupe remained in Paris. Paul Gauguin urgently wrote to Emile Bernard, "I have been to Buffalo's [Wild West Show]. You must make all efforts to come to see it. It is of enormous interest." And so were the Hindu dancers in the Javanese village and the stunning replica of the Cambodian Temple of Boro-Budur near the Champs de Mars. In November, Edvard Munch wrote to his father about the show, mentioning especially Buffalo Bill's duel with Chief Yellow Hand:

Sunday I was at Bilbao Bill's [sic]. Bilbao Bill is the most renowned trapper in America. He has come here with a large number of Indians and trappers and has set up an entire Indian village

outside Paris with many Indian tents. Bilbao Bill took part in several Indian wars . . . among other things in a big fight with a well-known Indian chief and took his scalp with a knife. The knife and the scalp are displayed in his tent. Many of the Indians that took part in the battle are here now and re-enact how it took place.

Munch's father answered on November 10 in what was to be his last letter, "It must be fun to see Indians, but I am doubtful if Mr. Bill really is an old trapper and that there is any trace of truth in the knife's and scalp's authenticity."

Then there were the American artists—Whistler and Sargent—who received the Legion of Honor, with prizes also showered on W. M. Chase, Childe Hassam, Eastman Johnson, and F. A. Bridgman, to name a few.

The most assiduous artistic visitor, however, was certainly RB, whose accounts of her almost daily sketching sessions re-

Rosa Bonheur: *Rocky Bear and Red Shirt.* Oil, 1890. Knoedler, New York. ❧ A week after the grand opening of Buffalo Bill's Wild West Show, Chief Red Shirt's squaw presented a jubilant Paris with its first native-born "papoose." Large numbers of newlyweds, still in white, rushed to the show in the hope of getting to touch the infant—a guarantee of a lifetime of happiness, according to an ancient Indian myth. Chief Red Shirt became Bonheur's favorite Indian model.

flect her enormous enthusiasm. Through her dealers the Tedescos and Mr. Knoedler, she had got permission from Buffalo Bill to work daily and wherever she chose.

> I was thus able to examine their tents at my ease. I was present at family scenes. I conversed as best I could with warriors and their wives and children. I made studies of the bisons, horses, and arms. I have a veritable passion, you know, for this unfortunate race and I deplore that it is disappearing before the White usurpers.

It is estimated that at least seventeen paintings and countless sketches emerged from RB's happy concourse with the "unfortunate race." Six of them were paintings of buffalos fleeing prairie fires or being attacked by Indians, and the rest were studies of mounted Indians. There was also an important portrait of Buffalo Bill himself mounted on his favorite white horse. This painting was widely reproduced on playbills, postcards, and posters and, at least in America, was RB's most widely known painting after *The Horse Fair*. There are several photographs extant of RB sketching and painting at the encampment, one of which shows her at work on the portrait wearing a black bonnet and voluminous skirts. Buffalo Bill's account of his meeting with RB mentions the portrait:

> While in the vicinity of Paris I accepted an invitation from Rosa Bonheur to visit her at her superb château. In return I extended her the freedom of the show, and she made many studies from life of the fine animals I had brought over with me. She also painted a portrait of me on my favorite horse—a picture which I immediately sent home to my wife.

Some commentators suggest that Buffalo Bill was not entirely satisfied with the portrait and had the head repainted, but there is another story that when he was informed that his North Platte, Nebraska, home was on fire, he wired immediately, "Save the Rosa Bonheur and let the flames take the rest."

For her part, RB always spoke of Buffalo Bill's visit to Fontainebleau with the same awe and delight which infused her accounts of the visits of royalty. She described how she seized the

(OPPOSITE, ABOVE) Rosa Bonheur at Buffalo Bill's headquarters. Paris, 1889. ⚜ Standing from left to right: Rocky Bear, Colonel Cody, art dealers Knoedler and Tedesco, Red Shirt, and William Irving, interpreter. Seated: Rosa Bonheur. Signed "To Roland Knoedler, Compliments of W. F. Cody."

(OPPOSITE, BELOW) Rosa Bonheur: *Buffalo Hunt.* Oil, 1889. The Tempel Smith Collection (40 × 58.5 cm). ⚜ Rosa spent weeks sketching at Buffalo Bill's thirty-acre campground near the Bois de Boulogne and made a series of drawings from which came all of her American West paintings of the 1890s.

Years later, when Buffalo Bill was visiting the Reinhardt Picture Gallery in Chicago, he was shown a small Bonheur painting of a buffalo. "Why that's my buffalo Barney, the old son-of-a-bitch," the Colonel said.

(RIGHT) *"I'm Coming."* Lithograph, 1905 (artist unknown). Courtesy Buffalo Bill Historical Center, Cody, Wyoming. ❧ One of a number of posters advertising Cody's arrival in Paris.

(BELOW) *Napoleon, Bonheur, and Buffalo Bill.* Lithograph, 1898. Courier Lithographic Co., Buffalo, New York. Courtesy: Library of Congress, Washington, D.C. ❧ With her back to a paunchy and brooding Napoleon, Bonheur rivets her artistic attention on her dashing model, the fabled Indian scout from the Yellowstone.

Bonheur had a large collection of William Henry Jackson's photographs of Indians and Western landscapes in her atelier which she used for study, along with other reproductions of views of the American West. "Your great American painter, Mr. Bierstadt of New York, has had the generosity to lend me several studies," she wrote Anna Klumpke in 1898.

occasion to offer him the two wild and untameable mustangs sent to her by Arbuckle. A few days later Buffalo Bill sent two cowboys who displayed their prowess with lassos, subduing even Apache, the wilder of the two. He was led peaceably to the railroad station much to RB's astonishment. She always recounted the story with relish.

The studies she had made during the seven months at the Indian encampment served RB for the rest of her life. She continued painting scenes from the Wild West, many of which had been commissioned by her faithful collectors in the United States. As late as 1895 she was asking Anna Klumpke if she could manage on her next trip to America to pick some wild sagebrush in order that she could complete her painting of wild horses fleeing a prairie fire. In her earlier years the romances of Walter Scott—the mythologies of kilted heroes and the magic of Scottish mists—had dominated her imagination. At the end of her life Scott was displaced by the romance of the American West.

17.
The Artist at Home

After the Franco-Prussian war, Rosa Bonheur settled into an even more regulated routine of work. There was no decline in her commissioned sales, although they still came mostly from England and the United States. England was particularly cordial. Camille Pissarro wrote disgustedly during his visit in 1871, "Here there is no art; everything is a question of business," while Théodore Duret shortly after wrote, "The English, with regard to French painters, like only Gérôme, Rosa Bonheur, etc. Corot and the other great painters don't exist for them as yet. Things here are the way they were twenty-five years ago in Paris."

RB's dealers in Paris—M. Tedesco and his three sons and Gambart—and, in London, Gambart's nephew Lefevre, were still very busy lining up commissions for her and pressing her for stock. This seemed to suit RB, and well into the 1890s she was writing to friends with evident satisfaction that she had to deliver a portrait of a dog here, a stag there, and various specifically ordered subjects. Many of these later works found their way into American collections. From the first success of *The Horse Fair* Gambart had kept up a steady exhibition schedule. Beween 1857 and 1867 he had shown six large collections of British and French contemporary art (working with the dealer Knoedler in New York) and almost always starred works of RB. He also looked after the brisk sales of RB's printed reproductions.

RB had her public, and they were grateful that there was little

The Bonheur residence, the Château de By. ❧ "I am an old rat," Rosa Bonheur wrote in 1867 when she was forty-five, "who after sniffing about over hill and dale retires quite satisfied to his hole, yet in reality somewhat sad to have seen the world without taking part in it."

evolution in her work after the mid-1850s. Her task of rendering the character of animals was faithfully undertaken in the same detailed, realistic manner she had developed after her English trip. Occasionally she was led by her youthful enthusiasm for romantic authors to undertake allegorical subjects, but these fell woefully short of her intentions and did not find favor even with her most faithful collectors. She was a reader of various romantic authors whose works, such as those of Eugène Sue, appeared in newspaper installments, and from time to time she was inspired by their subjects. Sue's story of the Godolphin Arabian, for instance, gave her the subject for her painting of battling horses which she struggled with for years. She also attended the theater occasionally and drew upon the themes of the popular playwrights of the day. "I have always loved the drama and even the melodrama. It helps and rests you at the same time."

RB was patently pleased with her ability to earn her living handsomely with her art, but there is considerable evidence that she was painfully sensitive to the fact that her reputation languished in France. As early as 1867, when Eugène de Mirecourt, a popular biographer of contemporary celebrities, was working on his monograph of her, the French resistance to RB's simple approach was apparent. Although he wrote sympathetically,

(UPPER RIGHT) Rosa Bonheur: *Calf's Head.* Oil, undated. Collection Rita Norrie Wells (47 × 39 cm). ⚜ Works such as this one might well have prompted one critic's high praise: "Mlle. Bonheur paints almost like a man."

(UPPER LEFT) Rosa Bonheur: *The Duel.* Pencil sketch, ca. 1894. Musée National du Château de Fontainebleau. ⚜ "A happy coincidence put into my hands an old engraving by Stubbs which allowed me to trace an authentic portrait of this hero," wrote Bonheur. "The white horse is none other than the Arabian, Godolphin, ancestor of all the great English stallions." This is Bonheur's preliminary study for a painting based on a popular eighteenth-century account of the Godolphin Arabian's victorious combat with the great black stallion of England, Hobgoblin.

(LEFT) Studio wall. ⚜ "I have a great mind to eat up all my sheep, to have all my dogs shot, except Shorck with the mange," wrote a despondent Rosa, irked with all her possessions and household responsibilities, "to leave my house as it is and to start off with nothing but my box of colors and a few articles of linen no woman can do without—not even savages. Bah! my dear Juju—the fit will pass."

Mirecourt expressed in his tactful way the general opinion of the more enlightened artistic circles in Paris:

> One would impute neither passion nor audacity, nor an excess of brilliance to her. Never did she dream of the unknown; never was she tempted by the extraordinary.... All her paintings are naïvely felt and scrupulously executed.

During the same year several other critics, including the prominent former admirer Thoré-Burger, remarked on her dryness, her tendency to imitate the English *animaliers*, and her spiritless technique. Thoré-Burger had long since moved on to the younger generation, among them Monet and Renoir, whom he praised in his review of the Salon and the Exposition Universelle of 1867. Ever since the Emperor had bowed to the protests of the new generation and had authorized the sensational Salon des Refusés in 1863, the young painters who would eventually be grouped under the label of "Impressionists" had been gaining ground with the critics. Some of them, such as Sisley, Monet, Renoir, and Bazille, were actually working near RB's retreat at Fontainebleau where they met and listened to the counsels of the old Barbizon painters Diaz and Millet. Although the Salon jury still included the staunch Second Empire favorites Gérôme and Cabanel, whom RB admired, the system after the Salon des Refusés had opened to admit elected jurors such as Daubigny and Corot and, through them, a few of the younger generation of open-air painters. All this attracted increasingly favorable attention to the rebellious generation and made RB's position even more difficult in her native country.

Stung by the French rebuffs, she withdrew more and more into her routine at By, and after 1875 into the charms of the fashionable social milieu in Nice near her protector, Gambart. In her letters to friends during this period there are hints that the criticism directed against her was taken as a personal attack on her private life with Nathalie.

Sometimes RB appeared to have an equivocal attitude toward the gibes the world sent her way. She liked to emphasize her masculinity at times, as for instance in the 1880s in Nice when she wore breeches on sketching trips. She wrote to her sister in 1884 that it amused her to see how puzzled people were:

> They wonder to which sex I belong. The ladies especially lose themselves in conjectures about "the little old man who looks so lively." The men seem to conclude, "Oh, he is some aged singer from St. Peter's at Rome who has turned to painting in his declining years to console himself for some misfortune."

That she did indeed look like a little old man is confirmed by the writer Jules Claretie who frequented By during RB's later years. He describes her elaborate studio and her store room and says:

> Amid the splendid confusion she quietly passed to and fro, and attired in a simple white blouse, with hair in crimps, she resembled indeed, as many beside myself have noted, that other master naturalist, the poetic painter of silver mornings and mysterious evenings, Père Corot.

Although in many ways RB called attention to her eccentric appearance, she was not always entirely pleased with the slighting references to her comic semblance. She always said her favorite book was *Don Quixote*, and in her numerous references to the Don it is clear that she identified with him—his misunderstood nobility and his propensity for encounters that always ended with his being thoroughly drubbed. Her stance in relation to a world that did not acknowledge her talents was generally one of puzzled mistrust. She tended to stay within her own circle of admiring friends, taking care to keep away from prying Parisian eyes. In her last years she lived close to her animals, working in the fields and forest or in her atelier at By. A friend described RB's elaborate arrangements to stay close to her subjects. She had built a bizarre little gig for painting outdoors in inclement weather, "a sort of little shepherd's wagon, a kind of cabin on four wheels standing in the middle of a field. . . . One side of this strange vehicle was all in glass, behind which, protected from cold air, sat Rosa Bonheur."

Renouard: *Cartoon of Rosa Bonheur. Revue encyclopédique,* 1896. ✤ Appearing at the time of the Russian royal tour of the Louvre, this humorous sketch portrays the only woman among the group of artists chosen by the Minister of Fine Arts to accompany the visiting sovereigns through the galleries. His choice was limited to painters and sculptors who had received the Officer of the Legion of Honor rosette.

(ABOVE) Stables. ❧ "She liked horses as much as she did dogs, and every day, when her work was done," recalled her friend Paul Chardin, "she harnessed and mounted her old mare, Margot."

(RIGHT) Rear door to gardens and stables.

(ABOVE) Rosa Bonheur, cigarette, and deer. Ca. 1898. ⚜ Bonheur would often ask herself the same question that most good zoo keepers trouble over: "In short, while caring for my animals so passionately, do I not displease them supremely since I deprive them of their liberty?"

(RIGHT, ABOVE) Velvet jacket (with Legion of Honor rosette), blouse, hat, shoes, and leggings; (BELOW) saddle. ⚜ "She always wished to have sole care of her heavy hunting boots," Bonheur's nephew said of her hunting habits. "She would always grease them herself, declaring that 'nobody else knew how to do it thoroughly and properly.' In the chase, as in many other things, 'Style makes the man,' she would insist."

As RB moved away from the Parisian art world she developed strong antipathies. The gossipy Goncourt brothers, for instance, excited her most profound distaste. As her friend Chardin tactfully remarked, she had a particular aversion for fashionable men. She had met the brothers sometime in 1859 and felt immediately that they were "endeavoring to make her talk." When her friend Louis Passy wrote asking her to receive them in her studio, she answered that she didn't wish to but would since she "knew the ways of the world and what she owed herself too well to let them see her real feelings for them." Chardin says she felt the Goncourts reciprocated, and she was right. In their journals the brothers referred to her nastily as "that Jewess," and years later RB was still bridling; she could not forget their superior airs, and in 1888 she wrote to a friend, Mme. August Cain:

By the way, dear Mme. Cain, if you chance to know Jules de Goncourt, please tell him for me that his poetic art, judging from

For half a century Bonheur squirreled away hundreds of sketches and studies in her big studio. "It is by their help that I pass judgment upon myself," she would say. "I compare my works, and I try not to slip backwards."

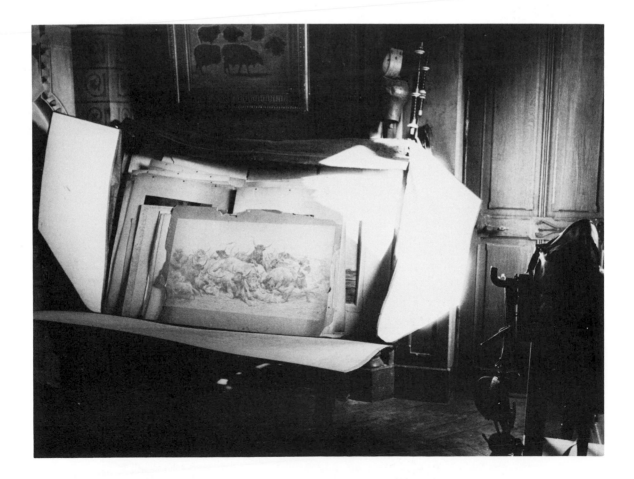

the few glimpses I have caught of it, is stunning. Hurrah for the Ideal! It inspires one as *La Juive* at the opera. And so, in the future, instead of painting animals head to front, I'll present them the other way about.

The letter continues in this sarcastic vein, deriding the "modern style" in which she imagined the Goncourts wrote. She kept a safe distance from everything relating to the "modern style." Her first exposure had been to the modern approach of the Barbizon painters, and even then, in her youth, she had shied away from contact with it. After that, each new onslaught on the *juste-milieu* academicism seemed to intimidate her and brought forth arch, even coy comments. The "realists," following in Courbet's wake, offended her vision of art as determined by Lammenais. The open-air painters, later called Impressionists, seemed to her to be mere daubers and often mere sensationalists. Her views on painting remained those instilled by her father, augmented by her experiences in England and Scotland. She tried to sum up her views at the end of her life in her dictated memoirs.

> The point of departure must always be a vision of the truth. The eye is the route of the soul, and the pencil or brush must sincerely and naïvely reproduce what it sees. Never forget that a dry line like a rod of iron doesn't exist in nature. Each object is surrounded by its own atmosphere.

At the same time she added, "I follow the thoughts of Schiller, who declared that if man has something to give to art, it is himself, and that which he registers outside himself must be reborn in him."

Her vaguely romantic philosophy was bolstered by a firm belief in the importance of technique and a feeling that she was preserving real values by adhering to strict technical procedures. She took great care to let her underpaintings dry thoroughly in the old-master way, and she used all mediums very sparingly for fear that they would affect her paintings in the future. She was finicky about her brushes, washing them with ritual care every day, and she kept a number of palettes carefully chosen to absorb excess oil. Her strong belief in the efficacy of her tech-

Corner of studio. ❧ "An animal painter must devote a good part of his existence not only to the training of his hand, but also to the collecting and the collaboration of all the observations he has made," Rosa advised Anna Klumpke. "It is a matter of long and serious study—a study that must be a component of life itself. If I had allowed this prolonged and incessant study to slip away from me for a more speedy acquisition of a few gold pieces, I should have indeed condemned myself to stagnate in idleness when the winter of my life began."

(ABOVE) Pillow embroidered with the Cross of the Legion of Honor. ❧ "Now I am turned 73 and have only one tooth left wherewith to snarl at humanity. However, my honors console me and I have no reason to complain," Bonheur wrote to a friend upon receiving the rank of "Officier" in 1894.

(RIGHT) "After dinner, I would go over to Rosa Bonheur's," reminisced Paul Chardin, "and finish the evening in her studio, both of us sitting before the burning logs in her big fireplace. . . . She would touch upon all conceivable topics, ranging from subjects for future pictures to questions of philosophy. Sometimes she would interrupt the gravest discussion with an unexpected sally or some schoolboy prank." The life-size male and female hunting dogs supporting the chimney were carved by Rosa's brother Isidore. To the right of the mantel hangs a portrait of Sophie Bonheur by her husband; at the left is a portrait of Madame Micas.

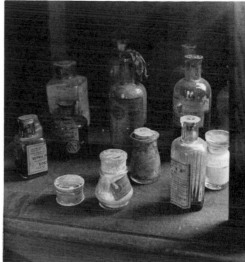

(ABOVE, RIGHT) Jars of mediums and pigments.

(ABOVE, LEFT) "She was very particular in the care of her palettes, some of which were kept perfectly clean, while others were covered with numerous coatings of mixed colors," wrote Rosa's close friend Consuelo Fould, an artist herself. "She thought a great deal of these palettes, which absorbed the oil and enabled her to better judge certain effects."

(LEFT) Plaster casts of gazelle and stuffed hawks in RB's studio. ❧ "Another excellent practice is to observe the aspect of plaster models of animals, especially to copy them by lamplight, which gives more distinctness and vibration to the shadows. . . . I owe all that I know to those patient and conscientious exercises."

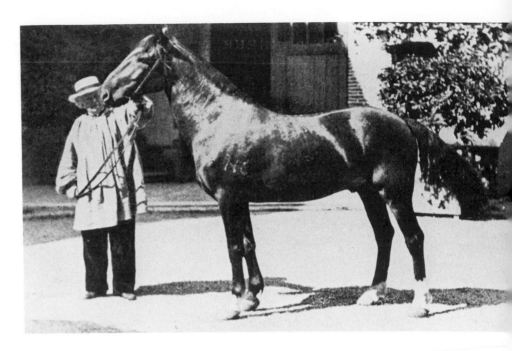

Rosa Bonheur with Solferino. Photographed at By, 1887.
❦ "Indeed, her accidents with horses were fairly frequent," recalled RB's friend Alexandre Jacob. "Right up to the very last, she insisted upon driving, and in several of her spills she managed to get considerably bruised. Of course, when she mounted horseback, she disdained a sidesaddle and rode like a man."

Jean Baptiste Claude Eugène Guillaume: *La Medaille d'Honneur et "Le Bouguereau des Vaches."* Caricature, 1899.
❦ "It would be ridiculous if the little painting I exhibited this year received such a high award."

niques is reflected in her slighting remarks about the Impressionists:

The Impressionists imagine that with their exaggerated facture they can impose themselves on the public. Believe me, one can paint with no matter what and no matter how, only you must have the art of never showing the secrets of the métier.

In a letter to Gambart, she condescendingly modifies her judgment: "Let's not make too much fun of the Impressionists. There are some good ones. . . . In my opinion all painters, important and less important, are impressionists, with the exception of the impossibilists and the quacks."

Rosa Bonheur reserved her outright admiration for those Second Empire favorites who had come into prominence during her youth and had remained faithful to the practice of pleasing rather than scandalizing the bourgeoisie. She maintained respect for Troyon, who along with Bracassat had been credited with introducing the Dutch landscape manner to France and who had, in 1849, received a first class medal from Louis Napoleon, which would insure his future. Troyon's naturalistic accuracy pleased RB, but it brought Baudelaire to cite Troyon in 1859 as "the finest example of skill without soul," rejecting, as he always did, the landscapists who had abandoned the romantic interpretive vision in favor of "truth." Baudelaire had even criticized Théodore Rousseau for the same fault. He granted that Rousseau had a sincere love of light and rendered it very well, but said he fell "into the famous modern fault which is born of a blind love of nature and nothing but nature."

RB too was often accused of having "skill without soul," but she herself was convinced that she was interpreting rather than recording nature, adhering to the dictates of her father and the soulful utopian writers he admired. All the same, she was fully a product of the Second Empire, and her associations were mainly with those artists who had remained safely ensconced in the salon tradition. In 1895, when she had been made an *officier* of the Legion of Honor, she expressed her satisfaction that a dinner in her honor would be attended by Bonnat, Detaille, and Gérôme—all painters whose fortunes had been secured during the Second Empire and whose styles pleased the middle classes well into the next century.

The criticisms leveled increasingly at RB after her retreat to By were partly based on her successes abroad, partly because of her obviously privileged connections with Louis Napoleon's court, and partly because of her idiosyncrasies and suspected lesbianism. But there was still another strange source of the negative response, going back to her father's old Saint-Simonian associations. During the late nineteenth century there were rumors that Rosa Bonheur was a Jew—and this at a time when anti-Semitism in France was finding vigorous and implacable proponents. This rumor held fast, and as late as the 1911 edition of the Encyclopedia Britannica, it was claimed that her real name was Rosa Mazel-Tov (a Hebrew translation of Bonheur) and that her father, Raymond, had attended synagogue. At the time that the Goncourt brothers referred to her as "that Jewess," anti-Semitism, even in enlightened circles, was becoming not only acceptable but fashionable. To call her a Jewess was to indicate their greatest contempt.

Although it is impossible to locate the source of the rumor, or to establish its veracity (she was, after all, born in Bordeaux, one

Rosa Bonheur: *Boniface*. Oil, ca. 1885. Klumpke. ⚜ This little study depicts one of RB's pet monkeys, which were always given the full run of the house. RB was quick to report their latest mischiefs to her friends. In 1888 she wrote this note: "Ratata is at liberty on the roof and in the garden. In the evening she comes home and does up my hair. I think she takes me for an old male of her kind!"

(RIGHT) Rosa Bonheur: Sketches on the theme "Haymaking in the Auvergne." Pencil, undated. Collection Mr. and Mrs. Warren Brandt (32 × 24 cm). ❧ Many of RB's sketches from her notebooks were sold at the Petit Gallery auction in 1900 carrying her studio stamp as signature.

(BELOW) Studio stamp. ❧ The paintings, studies, and drawings not signed by the artist carried these stamps at the Bonheur auction in Paris in 1900.

of the oldest and largest communities of Jews in Europe), it is likely that the idea gained currency because of her lifelong friendships with her father's Saint-Simonian colleagues, several of whom became prominent, even though they were Jews, during the Second Empire.

The Saint-Simonians, unlike the other Utopian sects of the period, favored Jews. They did so probably because Olinde Rodrigues from Bordeaux was one of Saint-Simon's most fervent disciples and became the chief organizer of the Saint-Simonians after the master's death. Rodrigues had been barred from the Ecole Normale Supérieure because he was a Jew and had attended instead the Polytechnicum, where other young Jews had

Writing table in RB's studio.
❀ "She would write charming epistles, merry and mad, sometimes, and always witty," her friend Georges Cain reminisced after Bonheur's death, ". . . and if she had not had warm attachments, her letters would have been far fewer."

Candid and colorful, Rosa's extensive correspondence—with its disheveled grammar and energetic handwriting—often enclosed little visual postscripts such as these.

BONHEUR [MARIE ROSALIE], ROSA (1822–1899), French painter, was born at Bordeaux on the 22nd of March 1822. She was of Jewish origin. Jacques Wiener, the Belgian medallist, a native of Venloo, says that he and Raymond Bonheur, Rosa's father, used to attend synagogue in that town; while another authority asserts that Rosa used to be known in common parlance by the name of Rosa Mazeltov (a Hebrew term for " good luck," *Gallice* Bonheur). She was the eldest of four children, all of whom were artists—Auguste (1824–1884) painted animals and landscape; Juliette (1830–1891) was " honourably mentioned " at the exhibition of 1855; Isidore, born in 1827, was a sculptor of animals. Rosa at an early age was taught to draw by her

Bonheur entry in the Encyclopaedia Britannica, 1911 edition. ⚜ Rosa Bonheur, twelve years after her death, her reputation on the wane, was listed in the Encyclopaedia Britannica as being of Jewish parentage. However, none of her family birth records gives proof to this speculation.

also found refuge. It was there he had met Saint-Simon, and there he recruited some of his Jewish friends, among them Gustave d'Eichthal and Isaac and Emile Pereire. They, together with Achille Fould, became prominent among the financial experts who guided Louis Napoleon's attempts to develop Saint-Simonian schemes for railroad and shipping routes. RB remained in regular contact with these old friends of her father, joining d'Eichthal for horseback rides in the Bois and becoming very close to the Achille Fould family. When the old Saint-Simonians assumed positions of power in later years they assisted RB in her relations to the court, probably even initiating the steps that brought her official honors. Toward the mid-1880s there was an overt attack on Jews in the form of Edouard Drumont's virulent pamphlet in 1886, and with it a growth of rightwing activity that very nearly toppled the republic a year later and brought forth an expression of distress from RB. The tide of anti-Semitism culminated in the Dreyfus affair, and brought with it ugly calumnies against the erstwhile Saint-Simonians. Anyone such as Rosa Bonheur who remained closely associated with them was tarred with the same brush.

18.
The End of an Era

The last momentous event in RB's life was the appearance of Anna Elizabeth Klumpke, an American painter born in San Francisco and educated in Paris. The affection RB had once lavished on Nathalie Micas was now transferred to Klumpke, much to the Bonheur family's distress. Eventually RB made Klumpke her sole heir, defying family and friends and the opinion of the world. The nature of their relationship was politely referred to as "friendship" in most of their correspondence, but Klumpke in her written works leaves little doubt of the passionate love she had inspired in the aged painter. In a few letters to very intimate friends, RB herself referred to Klumpke as "my wife."

Klumpke was the daughter of an ambitious mother who had brought her four daughters and son to Paris to compensate for a provincial early childhood in San Francisco. Even before they departed from America, Mrs. Klumpke had plied her children with culture. Among other things, she had given her tiny daughter a newspaper illustration of *The Horse Fair* and a small doll dressed like Rosa Bonheur. The family prospered in Paris. Anna, the eldest child, attended the Académie Julian, where she was a conscientious student and even won an honorable mention in the Salon of 1885. Her sisters also thrived: Augusta went to medical school and became a prominent physician; Dorothea became an astronomer of international repute and was for many years an official at the Paris Observatory; and Julie, the youngest, became a professional violinist.

As a child Anna had had a serious accident which left her per-

(ABOVE) Anna Klumpke: *Elizabeth Cady Stanton.* Oil, 1889. National Portrait Gallery, Washington, D.C. ✤ This portrait of the American reformer and feminist was painted by Klumpke in Paris the year so many other famous foreigners were lured there by the Exposition Universelle. Coincidentally, her son, Theodore Stanton, was the author of the book *Reminiscences of Rosa Bonheur,* published in 1910.

(OPPOSITE) Anna Klumpke: *Portrait of Rosa Bonheur.* Oil, 1898. Metropolitan Museum of Art, New York. Gift of the artist in memory of Rosa Bonheur, 1922. ✤ "Miss Anna, you are amazing!" chided Rosa while posing for her young American artist-companion. "In order to paint my mouth, my eyes, and my hair, you have me put on my jacket! Do the buttons of my jacket give you inspiration? That is what happens when you have not made enough preliminary studies; the imagination does not develop itself."

Anna Klumpke at work in the Bonheur studio. Photograph taken by Rosa Bonheur, 1898. ⚜ "I wish you could have painted me some years earlier," Rosa told Anna Klumpke. "But never mind, do the best you can now."

manently lame. Her long nose, which RB compared playfully to Cyrano's, and her pronounced lameness had apparently left her little illusion as to her marital future, and she had resolutely set out to make a solitary career as a portrait painter. A moderate success attended her efforts, and she began commuting between France and America painting commissioned portraits. According to her reminiscences, her dearest wish had always been to meet Rosa Bonheur, her childhood model and inspiration. The wish was granted when she was asked to serve as interpreter for John Arbuckle, president of the Royal Horse Association, the man who had sent RB the gift of wild American horses. There had been some confusion as to the source of the gift, and Arbuckle had never been thanked, so he asked for an audience with RB in 1889. He was invited to lunch at By and brought along Klumpke as interpreter. According to Klumpke, the day was marked by RB's immediate warm interest in her. For the next few years the two remained in touch. On one of her trips to America, Klumpke attempted, at RB's specific request, to ship back some weeds and sagebrush from the great plains of the West. Because this was unsuccessful, RB invited her again to lunch in 1895 and again requested, as Klumpke reports, "with that delicious naïveté characteristic of the foreigner unfamiliar with conditions over the vastness of the United States," that Klumpke pick a few bunches of fresh sagebrush for her.

Klumpke again obliged. On a cross-country train trip, she asked that the conductor halt the train in the desert so that she might pluck some plant specimens for Rosa Bonheur. Luckily she had encountered a rare conductor, for he complied with alacrity, explaining that he often stopped at the Metropolitan Museum to see *The Horse Fair*. He halted the train in mid-desert and, along with dozens of other passengers, helped gather "these prickly monsters" for the great painter.

Three years later, Klumpke began RB's portrait at By, where she had been installed in RB's studio. The older painter's insistent request that Klumpke remain with her as a companion soon resulted in a correspondence with Klumpke's mother, whom RB attempted to persuade of her honorable intentions. When Mrs. Klumpke resisted, RB wrote promising that a "lawyer would

(LEFT) Rosa Bonheur and companion painting in Fontainebleau Forest. Ca. 1898. ❧ "See how the trees detach themselves from the sky in a vigorous green, yet they are wrapped in a bluish tone—the air circulating between their branches," Bonheur pointed out to Anna Klumpke. "I will produce this effect with Prussian blue and yellow ochre; in the shadows I will put a blue-gray."

(BELOW) Ernest Gambart, Rosa Bonheur, and Anna Klumpke at Nice, 1899. ❧ This is Rosa Bonheur's last "official" photograph. Flanked by her dealer on one side and her young American companion on the other, she is seen bedecked with all her honors.

Plaster head of horse. Rosa
Bonheur atelier, 1977.

arrange a situation." As she had done with the Micas family, RB
tried to make a business arrangement that would obviate nasty
gossip. Still the Klumpke family objected. On August 12, 1898,
RB took matters into her own hands and wrote to Mme.
Klumpke once again, this time announcing that she and Anna
had decided to "associate our lives." To Anna, RB said, "The
thing is decided, right? This will be a divine marriage of two
souls." Eventually the Klumpke family saw the advantage of the
arrangement for Anna and were finally reconciled, at least according to Anna. Mrs. Klumpke wrote to RB that she was glad
Anna would be "considered as a little sister," although with
characteristic candor and bluntness, RB had not in the least suggested that particular relationship in her rather imperious letters
to Mrs. Klumpke.

With Klumpke safely ensconced, RB began dictating her
memoirs. She explained that none of her previous biographers
had done justice to two aspects of her life: her love of her
mother, whom she thought Klumpke resembled, and her love of
Nathalie. Her superstitious reverence for her mother's memory
stirred strange emotions in the old painter, and she hinted that
perhaps Klumpke was in some way her new guardian angel. It
appears that this fancied physical resemblance between
Klumpke and RB's mother kindled her memories of her childhood. One of the many touching accounts of RB's renewed pre-
occupation with her early life concerned a visit the two women
made to Nice in 1899. The deposed Empress Eugénie had sent
for RB to come to lunch at her villa in Cap Martin. As Klumpke
relates it, RB regarded the invitation as almost a command:

> On the appointed day Mr. Gambart escorted RB on her visit to
> the Empress. The great artist wore her black velvet gown on
> which she had pinned not the rosette of the Officer of the Legion
> of Honor, which had been bestowed upon her by President Car-
> not, but the Cross of the Chevalier, the one which Empress
> Eugénie had personally presented to her in 1865.

The Empress received RB in deep mourning for her son Louis
who had been killed in ambush in Zululand. The two women
strolled about the garden, and while Eugénie wept over her son,

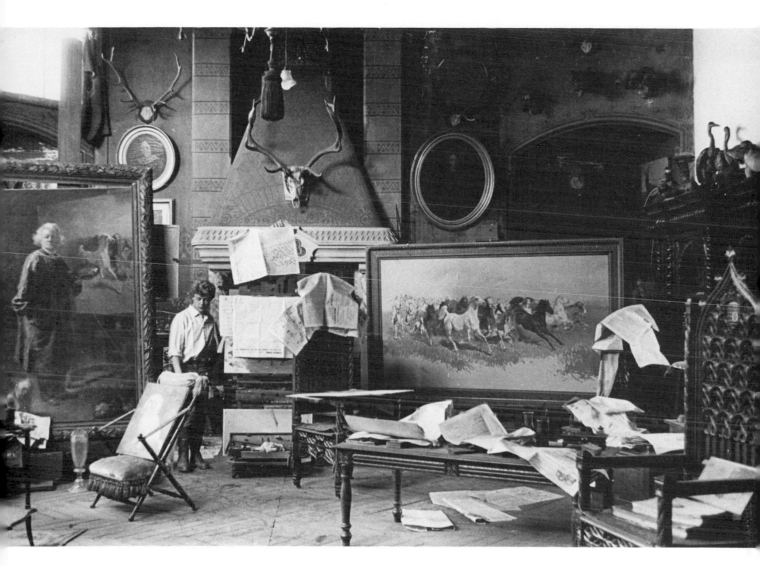

The studio at By. ❧ Bonheur's unfinished canvas of a galloping charge of wild horses is still on her easel; on the left, the last portrait of Bonheur, with her adored Charlie and Daisy by her feet, was painted by Anna Klumpke. Except for the signs of long neglect, the studio in 1977 looks much as it did at the time of Bonheur's death.

Last will. November 9, 1898. ❧ "I the undersigned Rosalie Marie given Rosa Bonheur artist and painter, sound of body and mind express here, fully my last wishes, owing nothing to anyone, and having no debts whatsoever, with my free will and of what I alone have earned by my work, having never had either lovers, or children. . . . I give and bequeath to Miss Anna-Elizabeth Klumpke, my companion and painter-colleague and my friend, all that I possess on the day of my death, appointing her my sole legatee. . . ."

RB wept for her long-lost mother. The visit ended with the Empress picking a flower and presenting it to RB, saying, "This is all I can offer you now."

Not only did Klumpke's presence bestir RB's earliest impressions, it also seemed to reinforce her most militant feminist sentiments. She had long associated Americans with a liberated attitude, as she told Klumpke repeatedly, and she talked at length and with occasional bitterness about her own position in a male-dominated society. Musing over the early biography by Mirecourt, she told Klumpke that his signaling the great influence of George Sand on her life was accurate, but his reference to Sand as "immoral" drew this response:

I don't think so. I venerate Mme. Sand, and have only one reproach to make against her. She was too womanly, too kind, and dropped the treasures of her noble heart and the pearls of her soul on the dung-heap, where cocks found the pearls and swallowed them without being able to digest them.

The happiness with Klumpke was short-lived. On May 25, 1899, after a brief bout with pneumonia, Rosa Bonheur died. She had instructed Klumpke to inscribe on her tomb, "Friendship is a divine affection." She had also rewritten her last will only shortly before her death. In the codicil she included sharp reproaches to her own family, who had not been any more cordial to her liaison with Klumpke than they had been to her earlier attachment to the Micas family. Judging from the hints in Klumpke's book and the silence of her other biographer, Stanton, there was considerable family acrimony after RB's death. In the earlier will of November 9, 1898, RB had already made Klumpke her legatee, the legacy comprising, notably:

My property at By in entirety . . . It is understood that furnishings, furniture, all that is in my house, cannot be removed and will belong to Anna-Elizabeth Klumpke, my decorations, finished and unfinished studies, paintings after these drawings, sketches, bronzes, horses and carriages, in a word, everything that exists in my ateliers as they are, as in my house, as well as my furniture in Paris. . . . I give and bequeath also to Mlle. Anna-Elizabeth Klumpke all my titles of revenue and values deposed in the hands of Messieurs Tedesco. . . .

(ABOVE) The list of names on the invitation to Rosa's funeral include her surviving brother, Isidore; a brother-in-law and sister-in-law; nephews and nieces and their children. Noticeably absent is the name of Anna Klumpke.

(ABOVE, LEFT) Memorial ribbons. ⚜ "To our Illustrious Honorary President—The Union of Women Painters and Sculptors"; "The City of Bordeaux"; "The Society of French Artists"; "The Town of Thomery"; "The National School of Decorative Arts" are among the many who sent their white and lavender taffeta mementos to Bonheur's funeral services.

(LEFT) Micas family vault, Père Lachaise cemetery, Paris. ⚜ "I want to be buried in the same vault as my friend Miss Nathalie-Jeanne Micas, since I have that right, having been her sole legatee and only heir and agreed upon between us. This vault belongs to me and is located in the Père Lachaise cemetery," Bonheur wrote in her last will. Anna Klumpke's ashes joined them in 1945.

In 1929 Anna Klumpke donated her vast Rosa Bonheur collection to the
Musée National du Château de Fontainebleau. Included in the gift was her
own last portrait of her mentor, with Charlie, Rosa's favorite Yorkshire
terrier.

At the time, a critic for *Studio International* wrote this dour comment
about the opening of the galleries: "One pictures her anatomically perfect
steeds prancing in time to the mixed strains of the American Music School
across the Court. Rosa Bonheur has so long been rated as a thoroughly mediocre painter that one suspects this sudden act of recognition comes less as
the result of any deep appreciation of her work than as a symptom of the
esoteric tendency to revive the horrors of the XIX century for the sake of
novelty."

The Rosa Bonheur Galleries have been closed to the public for a number
of years.

She also instructed Klumpke that her body be placed in the vault at Père Lachaise cemetery already occupied by Mme. Micas and Nathalie, and that the funeral ceremony be extremely modest. Her strictures were so carefully respected that her old friend and colleague Bouguereau, who had first met her at the rue d'Assas where he had gone to borrow a goat as a model for one of his paintings, was unable to deliver his funeral remarks. Excerpts from his undelivered eulogy included:

> The fame which for fifty years has encircled the name of this talented artist has been heightened by the mysterious charm which surrounded this woman, painter of wild and domestic animals, living retired from the the world among her dear models—virile, energetic, original, but modest and good. . . . Though her artistic life was passed among various phases of the modern schools, she always remained true to her own conceptions of art and acted only upon her inspirations. . . . The faithful worship of nature made her modest. . . .

Shortly before she died, RB had submitted work for the first time in forty years to the Salon. Although there were a few kind remarks, the response had been less than enthusiastic. Klumpke consoled her, promising that her true stature would emerge in the new biography. When obituaries appeared, there were many cool evaluations. *The New York Tribune* of May 27, 1899, praised her masterpiece, *The Horse Fair*, but added that when compared with the three or four great French artists who devoted themselves to animal portrayal she was compelled to take a lower rank:

> The explanation is simple. Rosa Bonheur was a competent painter, handling her brushes with skill and understanding her subjects, but she lacks the spark of genius which places a picture apart. In "The Horse Fair" there is impeccable truth and there is a certain beauty, but the charm of originality, distinction of style, is absent. She practised a kind of dignified realism. . . . In the jargon of the studios it would be said that she lacks "quality" . . .

Although RB had maintained the respect of her old colleagues, such as Bouguereau, her reputation had diminished as

"The crowd which thronged the Petit Gallery yesterday," reported the *New York Herald's* Paris edition of May 31, 1900, "when the sale of paintings and studies by Rosa Bonheur began, was of quite a special character, the room being filled with foreigners of all nationalities." The two-column story continued, "The best price were made for oxen. . . . The sheep and goats were less appreciated. . . . The foxes did not take."

far as the professional art world was concerned. In the twentieth-century, it slipped far enough so that the distinguished art historian John Rewald could say of *The Horse Fair* that it was "a majestic exercise in futile dexterity."

Collectors, however, were not troubled. When the contents of RB's studio were auctioned during a four-day sale in June 1900, they flocked to acquire her works at good prices. There were 1,835 entries in the auction catalog—892 paintings, 200 watercolors, 742 pastels and drawings, among them 255 studies of horses, 94 of dogs, 238 cows and bulls, 221 wild beasts, especially lions and tigers, 221 deer, 250 landscapes with animals, 50 miscellaneous works, and numerous studies of Indians. There were a few scandalous whispers concerning the sale and some dark hints that her dealers had rigged it. The British art dealer René Gimpel claimed in his autobiography that some six hundred paintings in her studio had been "finished" by her dealers

Rosa Bonheur: *Wheat Threshing in the Camargue.* Oil, ca. 1864–1899. Musée National de Château de Fontainebleau (313 × 654 cm). ❧ "My dream is to show the fire which comes out of the horses' nostrils; the dust which rises from their hooves. I want this to be an infernal waltz," was Rosa's description of her immense unfinished canvas, *La Foulaison du blé en Camargue,* which covered one of her studio walls for over thirty years. During the last year of her life Rosa struggled with the horses while Anna Klumpke worked on the ground and the sky. Bonheur died before the painting was completed.

before the sales. In any case, RB's sales continued to engage dealers well into the 1920s and even after. During the Second World War, for instance, a small, rather insignificant work was sold at auction in New York for the relatively high price of $7,600.

In some of the posthumous evaluations of Rosa Bonheur as a painter, there are justifiable confusions. After all, she often spoke as a fervent romantic, fancying herself a disciple of George Sand, whom she often quoted as having said, "Art for art's sake is a vain word. But art for the truth, art for the beautiful and the good, that is the religion I seek for." At the same time as she was idealistically seeking a religion of the beautiful and good, RB was following meticulously the scientific methods newly appreciated in mid-nineteenth-century France. RB clung to the romantic interests of her youth, reading Scott, Ossian, and Cervantes, but in her work she was a child of industry and

science. There had been the great Cuvier–Saint-Hilaire debate, it is true, and Geoffroy de Saint-Hilaire had captivated the creative personalities of his time with his emphasis on the philosophical and humanistic aspects of his science, but the very fact of the debate indicated how strongly the mechanistic forces were represented. Industrialism called forth its own terms, and they were far less humanistic than RB imagined. During the Second Empire, the emphasis on industry and even on mass production was always justified in the name of progress and science. RB herself sought scientific information constantly, and despite her imagined position as "interpreter" of individual animal characters, she tended to rely on practical data much as a scientist would. She fell into the routines of the newly industrialized society almost unconsciously. As a Second Empire success, she ran a kind of workshop and willingly supplied her middlemen with merchandise. Yet, in her own view, she maintained the early principles instilled in her by her father and enunciated by Lammenais. This ambivalence in her, of which she wasn't aware, early revealed itself and was particularly significant after she painted *The Horse Fair* and discovered the English *animaliers*. For the rest of her life she felt on firm ground only when she was studying her animals with a naturalistic intent. She could not move beyond the boundaries imposed by her methods. Happily, her techniques coincided with the culture sponsored by the Second Empire and permitted her to enjoy a renown unequaled even by the greatest of nineteenth-century painters. She could continue to think of herself as a disciple of Lammenais, but in fact she was the perfect exemplar of the pragmatic attitudes of the period in which she lived.

Inaugurated on May 19, 1901, on the Place Denecourt in Fontainebleau, the Rosa Bonheur Monument was a gift of Ernest Gambart. The huge bull was a full-size copy of an early small Bonheur sculpture, and it is flanked by three bronze reliefs of her most famous paintings made by her brother Isidore. This monument was never a favorite in this art-conscious town. Some citizens wanted it removed; others suggested that it be moved to the entrance of the local slaughterhouse. Pranksters often daubed it with red paint. Like a number of monuments to other famous figures of France, it was scrapped during the German occupation of France in 1941.

Chronology

1822   Born March 16 at 29 rue Saint-Jean-Saint-Seurin in Bordeaux, the first child of Raimond Oscar-Marie Bonheur, a painter and teacher, and Sophie Marquis, a musician. Given the name of Rosalie.

1824   A brother, Auguste, is born September 21.

1827   A second brother, Isidore, is born May 15.

1828   Father leaves for Paris to teach painting, with the intention of sending for his family as soon as he earns enough money
"Rosalie asks every day when you are coming back . . ." writes Sophie to her husband. "She is painting you some little men to send you."
Goya dies in exile in Bordeaux.

1829   After a two-and-a-half day journey by stagecoach, Sophie Bonheur arrives in Paris with her three young children to join her husband on rue St. Antoine, a bustling thoroughfare near Les Halles. Rosa's grandmother, Mémé Bonheur, goes along to help with the children.

1830   A sister, Juliette, is born a few days before the July Revolution.
Raimond Bonheur joins the Saint-Simonians and becomes an apostle/gardener at their monastery at Ménilmontant.
Rosa first makes the acquaintance of Nathalie Micas while playing in the gardens of the Place Royale.

1831   Raimond Bonheur's painting *A Pilgrim Without Shelter in the Storm* is accepted at the annual Salon.

1833   Sophie Bonheur dies of "exhaustion" at thirty-six and is buried in potter's field. Raimond Bonheur is left to care for his four young children alone, his mother having died two years earlier.

1834 Rosa earns her first pocket money coloring heraldic insignias, fashion engravings, and kaleidoscopic views for M. and Mme. Bisson, close friends of her father.

1835 After giving small attention to her school studies, Rosa ends her formal education at thirteen. She persuades her father to teach her drawing and painting in his studio.

1836 Begins copying the masters at the Louvre and is nicknamed "the little Hussar" because of her dress. Her favorites are Paulus Potter, Poussin, Porbus, Léopold Robert, Salvator Rosa, and Karel Dujardin.

Father is commissioned to paint the portrait of Nathalie Micas, the twelve-year-old daughter of an acquaintance of his. A close friendship develops between the two girls.

1838– Visits the Jardin des Plantes, farms, and stables in the nearby
1840 village of Villiers and the Veterinary School at Alfort to sketch animals.

1841 Exhibits for the first time in the Salon—a small oil, *Rabbits Nibbling Carrots*, and a drawing, *Goats and Sheep*, which she sells. Rosa is nineteen.

1842 Father marries Marguerite Picard Peyrol, a twenty-nine-year-old widow from the Auvergne. The family's nomadic existence ends. "In my youth," Rosa once remarked, "we used to migrate with the birds." They settle down at 13 rue Rumford, which is nearly in the country, close to the Monçeau Plain.

1844 Permanently changes her signature from Rosalie Bonheur to Rosa Bonheur.

1845 Exhibits six paintings at the Salon and is awarded a third-class medal. Baudelaire writes his first Salon review but does not mention Bonheur.

Rosa returns to Bordeaux to fetch her sister, Juliette, who has been boarding with Mme. Aymé, an old family friend, since their mother's death. Brings back a full sketchbook of drawings of the Landais countryside, its shepherds, and their flocks.

1846 Joins her father in giving drawing lessons to her brothers and sister. Urges them to become artists also. In September leaves for the Auvergne with her stepmother to visit her parents.

George Sand writes *The Devil's Pool* in four days.

1847   The critic Théophile Thoré publishes his "Salon" with praise for Rosa.

Travels to the Auvergne again.

1848   Louis-Philippe is overthrown in February during the three-day revolution and goes into exile.

Four members of the Bonheur family participate in the Salon: father, two brothers, and Rosa with eight works of her own. She receives a gold medal. The jury includes Delacroix, Meissonier, Corot, Ingres.

Goes on a visit with Nathalie to the Nivernais around the time of her half-brother Germain's birth. Makes many sketches of cattle of this region. Upon return to Paris rents her own studio at 56 rue de l'Ouest near the Luxembourg.

Works for many months on the large canvas *Ploughing in the Nivernais*, which had been commissioned by the government and was thought to have been inspired by George Sand's *The Devil's Pool*.

1849   Father dies on March 23 at fifty-three.

Rosa and her sister, Juliette, take over his directorship of the School of Drawing for Young Girls on rue Dupuytren.

Ploughing in the Nivernais is shown at the Salon; it captures the attention of the critics and brings Rosa her first major success. The Musée du Luxembourg buys it for 3000 francs and she is given a large Sèvres vase by the government.

The enterprising Tedesco brothers become her dealers.

1850   Rosa and Nathalie, who is in poor health, leave in early June on a four-month working holiday to the Pyrenees. Visit the spas, sketch, and go on a vulture hunt. Return to Paris only to take off for another cure to Ems, Prussia, almost immediately.

A second version of *Ploughing in the Nivernais* is sold to a M. Marc for 4000 francs, half of which Rosa shares with her brother Auguste for his participation in the painting.

1851   Coup d'état by Louis Napoleon.

Victor Hugo goes into exile.

Rosa frequents the horse market at Boulevard de l'Hôpital near l'Hospice de la Salpêtrière in preparation for her drawings of Percherons and their handlers. Begins wearing male attire to escape notice while at work there.

1852   Louis Napoleon becomes Emperor as Napoleon III.

1853   Shown at the Salon, *The Horse Fair* quickly becomes the fa-
        vorite of the art-going public and receives the praise of most
        critics.
        In celebration, Rosa and Nathalie take another journey to the
        south of France. During August and September they wander
        through the wilder craggy regions of the Pyrenees and meet
        up with some smugglers.
        Upon return to Paris they move into a spacious new studio at
        32 rue d'Assas with a tree-filled courtyard and stables,
        hutches, and roomy pens for their growing menagerie.

1854   The Crimean War is declared. England, France, and Turkey
        become allies against Russia.
        David d'Angers makes a bronze portrait medallion of Bonheur
        for his great artists series, "Galerie des Contemporains."

1855   *The Horse Fair* is bought by one of the leading dealers in Eu-
        rope, Ernest Gambart, for 40,000 francs. He plans to send it
        "traveling over the Kingdom" on exhibition in Britain and
        charge one shilling per viewer. She hurriedly paints a quar-
        ter-sized version of it to send to Thomas Landseer for an en-
        graving; shortly afterwards, Jacob Bell, an English collector,
        buys it for 25,000 francs.
        Haymaking in the Auvergne is shown at the Exposition Uni-
        verselle in Paris. She is awarded a gold medal, and the paint-
        ing is hung as a companion piece to *Ploughing in the
        Nivernais* at the Musée du Luxembourg.
        This is the last Salon Bonheur participates in with any regu-
        larity. Of the nearly fifty works she has shown in them over
        the past fifteen years, all have had an animal motif.

1856   Dines with Delacroix on February 10.
        Toward the middle of summer, at the invitation of her dealer
        Gambart, Rosa and Nathalie leave for London to make a
        grand tour of England and Scotland with him. They meet
        Queen Victoria, Edwin and Thomas Landseer, Sir Charles
        Eastlake, William Millais, John Ruskin, and other luminaries
        of the English aristocracy and art milieu.
        Engraving of *The Horse Fair* by Thomas Landseer is dedi-
        cated to Queen Victoria on July 21.

1857   Gambart sells *The Horse Fair* to an American entrepreneur,
        William P. Wright of Weehauken, New Jersey, with the un-
        derstanding that it be "toured" through the main cities of the
        East from New Orleans to Boston for at least two years.

1859   The small version of *The Horse Fair* is bequeathed to the National Gallery by the Jacob Bell estate. It disappears from public view for six years, turning up in RB's studio for the weaker parts to be retouched.

1860 Rosa and Nathalie, their life and studio overflowing with animals, collectors, and celebrity-hunters, jointly buy the Château de By, a manor house near the Forest of Fontainebleau, and take refuge there. Nathalie's mother moves in with them.

Resigns as co-director of the School of Drawing for Young girls.

1862 Napoleon III's Master of the Hounds, Baron Tristan Lambert, gives Bonheur permission to hunt in the Forest of Fontainebleau.

Gambart sues two London print dealers for selling pirated prints of *The Horse Fair*.

1863 Elected Honorary Member of the Pennsylvania Academy of Fine Arts in Philadelphia and of the Société des Artistes Belges.

Manet's *Luncheon on the Grass* is turned down by the Salon; it is shown at the "Salon des Refusés" instead.

On June 10, French troops arrive in Mexico City.

1864 Toward the end of June, Napoleon III and the Empress Eugénie invite Rosa to lunch at the Château de Fontainebleau.

1865 On June 10 the Empress Eugénie surprises Bonheur at her easel and gives her the ribbon of the Chevalier de la Légion d'Honneur. Bonheur is the first woman artist to receive it.

Her quarter-size version of *The Horse Fair* is finally hung at the National Gallery in London, the first painting exhibited there by a living artist.

Emperor Maximilian and Empress Carlotta award Bonheur the Cross of San Carlos of Mexico.

1867 After an absence of twelve years, Bonheur shows again in the Salon at the Exposition Universelle. Critics attack her for copying Landseer. Of the ten works exhibited, nine belong to English collectors and one to the Empress Eugénie.

Auguste Bonheur receives the Chevalier de la Légion d'Honneur as a result of his sister's intervention.

1868 Elected a Member of the Académie des Beaux-Arts of Antwerp.

Over the past fifteen years Gambart has bought twenty-one pictures from Bonheur for 284,000 francs.

1870   The Franco-Prussian War begins on July 19.

          The Horse Fair is bought at auction by A. T. Stewart, wealthy New York dry-goods merchant, who hangs it in one of the galleries of his newly built "marble palace" on the corner of Fifth Avenue and 34th Street.

1871   Paris is besieged by the Prussians. Bonheur sets to work painting studies of her animals with the notion of eating them before the Prussians descend on her village.

          The war ends on May 10.

1872   Begins series of works based on *les grands fauves*—panthers, lions, and tigers.

1874   On July 22 Samuel P. Avery, American engraver and art dealer and a founder of the Metropolitan Museum of Art, makes one of his buying trips to Bonheur's studio.

1875   Bonheur trades 5000 francs' worth of her work for the rental of a villa belonging to her dealer Gambart, in Nice. Owing to Nathalie's fragile health, they plan to winter there from now on.

1880   Gambart sends Bonheur two lions he has bought from a circus in Marseilles to add to her menagerie in By.

          From Alphonso XII of Spain she receives the Commander's Cross of the Royal Order of Isabella; from the King of Belgium, the Catholic Cross and the Leopold Cross.

1882   Germain Bonheur, her half-brother, landscape painter and pupil of Gérôme, dies at thirty-four.

          A painting by Cézanne is finally accepted in the Salon after he had been refused entry every year since the mid-60s. He is forty-three.

1884   Brother Auguste Bonheur, who has had a small success as an animal painter, dies of a heart attack in a railway car on February 21.

1885   Buys the Villa Bornala in Nice and builds a studio next to it. A street in the town is named after her, as is one for Queen Victoria.

          Elected Honorary Member of the Royal Academy of Watercolorists of London; also receives the Merit des Beaux-Arts de Saxe-Coburg-Gotha.

1887   On March 25 Samuel P. Avery, acting as agent for Cornelius Vanderbilt, buys *The Horse Fair* at the Stewart auction for $53,000 and donates it to the newly founded Metropolitan Museum of Art.

1889   Nathalie Micas dies at the Château de By on June 24.

On September 25 Buffalo Bill Cody comes to visit Bonheur at her studio while on tour with his Wild West Show in Paris during the Exposition Universelle. She paints his portrait on a white horse.

John Arbuckle, prosperous New York coffee merchant, comes to call on October 5, accompanied by Anna Klumpke, a young thirty-three-year-old American artist living in Paris. Arbuckle is anxious to see the three wild mustangs he had sent Bonheur from his ranch in Wyoming a few years earlier.

1890   President Carnot visits studio on September 15.

1891   Sister Juliette dies. Under Rosa's teaching, she too had become an animal painter.

Before sailing to Boston to paint some portraits, Anna Klumpke pays a second visit to Bonheur's studio.

1893   Bonheur exhibits four paintings at the Chicago Columbian Exposition: *King of the Forest, The Stampede, Sheep,* and *The Pastoral.*

1894   On April 3 Rosa Bonheur receives the award of Officier de la Légion d'Honneur, the first woman to achieve this rank.

1895   Anna Klumpke, upon her return from the United States, makes several visits to the Château de By.

Isidore Bonheur is awarded the Chevalier de la Légion d'Honneur as a sculptor. (The stone lions on the stairs of the Palais de Justice on Place Dauphine are his.)

1896   Is invited by the Ministre des Beaux-Arts to be one of the group of artists (all Légion d'Honneur confrères) chosen to escort the Tsar and Tsarina of Russia through the Louvre galleries.

1897   Exhibits four large pastels at the Petit Gallery in Paris and receives some favorable reviews.

1898   On June 11 Anna Klumpke arrives at Bonheur's studio to begin work on a portait of her. At the end of summer Anna is invited by Rosa to stay on indefinitely. She starts taking notes for a biography commissioned by her mentor.

On November 7 Bonheur draws up a will leaving everything to Anna.

1899   In late January Rosa and Anna spend ten days in Nice visiting Gambart at his palatial villa, Les Palmiers. Upon their return to By they build a new studio, in which they undertook to finish the huge painting *Wheat Threshing in the Camargue,* started some thirty-five years earlier.

On May 25, after a brief illness, Rosa Bonheur dies of a pulmonary congestion at 10:30 in the evening. She is seventy-seven. A few days later she is buried in Père Lachaise cemetery in the same crypt as her first companion, Nathalie Micas. Anna Klumpke's ashes would join them there in 1945.

—D.B.H.

Bibliography

Allemagne, Henri René d'. *Les Saints-Simoniens, 1827–1837*. Paris: Librairie Gründ, 1930.

——. *Prosper Enfantin et les grandes entreprises du XIX siècle*. Paris: Librairie Gründ, 1935.

Augé de Lassus, L. "Rosa Bonheur," *La Revue de l'Art*. Paris: April 1900.

Avery, Samuel P. *The Diaries 1871–1882 of Samuel P. Avery, Art Dealer*. Ed. Madeleine Fidell Beaufort, Herbert L. Kleinfield, and Jeanne K. Welcher. New York: Arno Press, 1979.

Bacon, Henry. "Rosa Bonheur," *Century* (London), October 1881.

Bizardel, Yvon. *American Painters in Paris*. New York: Macmillan, 1960. (Tr. Richard Howard)

Blanc, Louis. *The History of Ten Years, 1830–1840*. London: Chapman and Hall, 1844.

Boime, Albert. "The Case of Rosa Bonheur: Could a Victorian Woman Make Good Only as a Man?" (Unpublished manuscript)

Bolton, Sarah Knowles. *Lives of Girls who became Famous*. New York: Thomas Crowell and Co., 1886.

Bonheur, Rosa. "Fragments of My Autobiography," *Magazine of Art* (London), volume 26, 1902.

Bonnefon, Paul. "Une Famille d'Artistes, Raimond et Rosa Bonheur," *L'Art* (Paris), 1903–4.

Cahn, Théophile. *La vie et l'oeuvre d'Etienne Geoffroy de Saint-Hilaire*. Paris: Presses Universitaires de France, 1962.

Catlin, George. *Letters and Notes on the Manners, Customs, and Conditions of the North American Indians*, two volumes. London, 1841.

Claretie, Jules. "Rosa Bonheur—An Appreciation with Some Hitherto

Unpublished Studies," *Harper's Magazine* (New York), 1901.

Clark, T. J. *The Absolute Bourgeois.* London: Thames and Hudson, 1973.

Clement, Clara Erskine. *Women in the Fine Arts.* Cambridge: Houghton Mifflin and Co., 1904.

Cody, William F. *The Autobiography of Buffalo Bill.* New York: Rinehart, 1920.

Cole, Gordon D. H. *A History of Socialist Thought.* London: Macmillan, 1955.

Delacroix, Eugène. *The Journal of Eugène Delacroix.* New York: Covici Friede, 1937.

Demont-Breton, Virginie. "Rosa Bonheur," *Revue des revues* (Paris), 1899.

Duveau, Georges. *1848—The Making of a Revolution.* New York: Pantheon, 1967.

Eitner, Lorenz. *Géricault.* Los Angeles: Los Angeles County Museum of Art, 1971.

Ewers, John C. *Artists of the Old West.* Garden City: Doubleday, 1973.

Flaubert, Gustave. *Sentimental Education.* London: Penguin, 1964. (Tr. Robert Baldick)

Fontanges, Haryett. *La Legion d'Honneur et les Femmes Décorées.* Paris: Alliance Cooperative du Livre, 1905.

Gambart, Ernest. *Monument érigé en memoire de Rosa Bonheur à Fontainebleau.* Macon, 1901.

Geoffroy de Saint-Hilaire, Etienne. *Principes de Philosophie Zoologique.* Paris: Pichon et Didier, 1830.

Goncourt Brothers Journals. Ed. and transl. by George J. Becker. Ithaca, N.Y.: Cornell University Press, 1969.

Goodall, Frederick. *The Reminiscences of Frederick Goodall.* London: W. Scott, 1902.

Guedalla, Philip. *The Second Empire.* New York: Putnam, 1922.

Guérard, Albert. *Napoleon III.* Cambridge: Harvard University Press, 1943.

Harris, Ann Sutherland, and Nochlin, Linda. *Women Artists 1550-1950.* Los Angeles: Los Angeles County Museum of Art, and New York: Knopf, 1976.

Hervier, Paul-Louis. "Lettres inédites de Rosa Bonheur," *La Nouvelle Revue* (Paris), January–February 1908.

Hubbard, Elbert. *Little Journeys to the Homes of Famous Women, Book 1.* East Aurora, N.Y.: The Roycrofters, 1911.

Klumpke, Anna Elizabeth. *Memoirs of an Artist*, ed. Lilian Whiting. Boston: Wright and Potter, 1940.

———. *Rosa Bonheur, sa vie, son oeuvre*. Paris: Flammarion, 1908.

LaForge, Anatole de. *La Peinture Contemporaine en France*. Paris: Ayot, 1856.

Leigh, Jerrard. "Rosa Bonheur Revealed as a Painter of Westerns," *The Westerners Brand Book* (Chicago), August 1953.

Leonard, Elizabeth Jane, and Goodman, Julia Cody. *Buffalo Bill, King of the Wild West*. New York: Library Publishers, 1955.

Lepelle de Bois-Gallais, F. *Biography of Mademoiselle Rosa Bonheur*. London: 1857.

Maas, Jeremy. *Gambart—Prince of the Victorian Art World*. London: Barrie and Jenkins, 1975.

———. *Victorian Painters*. London: Putnam, 1969.

McCracken, Harold. *George Catlin and the Old Frontier*. New York: Dial Press, 1959.

Ménard, René. "French Artists of the Present Day." *Portfolio* (London), 1875.

Mirecourt, Eugène de. *Rosa Bonheur*. Paris: Librairie des contemporains, 1856.

Montrosier, Eugène. *Grands Peintres français et étrangers*. Paris: H. Launette, 1884–1886, volume 2, part 1

Morazé, Charles. *The Triumph of the Middle Classes*. New York: New York World, 1966.

Newhall, Beaumont, and Edkins, Diana E. *William H. Jackson*. Fort Worth: Amon Carter Museum, 1974.

Nochlin, Linda. "Why Have There Been No Great Women Artists?" *Art News* (New York), January 1971.

Petit, Georges, Galerie. *Atelier Rosa Bonheur*. Paris: G. Petit, 1900.

Peyrol, René. "Rosa Bonheur, Her Life and Work," *The Art Journal* (London), 1889.

Roger-Milès, Léon. *Rosa Bonheur: sa vie, son oeuvre*. Paris: Société d'édition artistique, 1900.

Rosenblum, Robert. "The 19th Century Franc Revalued," *Art News* (New York), Summer 1969.

Rossi, Paul A., and Hunt, David C. *The Art of the Old West—From the Collection of the Gilcrease Institute*. New York: Knopf, 1971.

Ruskin, John. *The Works of John Ruskin*, ed. E. T. Cook and Alexander Wedderburn. London, 1901.

Russell, Don. *Lives and Legends of Buffalo Bill*. Norman: University of Oklahoma Press, 1960.

St. John, Percy B. *The Three Days of February, 1848*. New York: Putnam, 1848.

Salinger, Margaretta. "Rosa Bonheur," *French Painting II*. New York: Metropolitan Museum of Art, 1966.

Sand, George. *The Devil's Pool*. The Harvard Classics, ed. William Allen Neilson. New York: Collier, 1917.

Sergeant, Philip W., B.A. *The Last Empress of the French*. Philadelphia: Lippincott, n.d.

Stanton, Theodore. *Reminiscences of Rosa Bonheur*. New York: Appleton, 1910.

————. *The Woman Question in Europe*. New York: Putnam, 1884.

Stanton, Theodore, and Blatch, Harriet Stanton. *Elizabeth Cady Stanton As Revealed in Her Letters, Diary, and Reminiscences*. New York: Harper, 1922.

Szajkowski, Zosa. "The Jewish Saint-Simonians and Socialist Anti-semites in France," *Jewish Social Studies*, New York, January 1947.

Tchou, Claude. *Guide de Fontainebleau Mysterieux*. Paris: Les Guides Noirs, 1967.

The Second Empire, Art in France under Napoleon III. Philadelphia: Museum of Art, 1978.

Vollard, Ambroise. *Paul Cézanne*. Paris: Crès, 1919.

Index